STAR WARS
WORKBOOKS

4TH GRADE MATH

FOR AGES 9–10

BY THE EDITORS OF BRAIN QUEST
CONSULTING EDITOR: BARBARA BLACK

WORKMAN PUBLISHING
NEW YORK

BRAIN QUEST and WORKMAN are registered trademarks of Workman Publishing, Inc.

Library of Congress Cataloging-in-Publication Data is available.

ISBN: 978-0-7611-8936-7

Workbook series designer Raquel Jaramillo
Designers Tim Hall, Claire Torres, Gordon Whiteside, Abby Dening
Writers Claire Piddock, Megan Butler
Editors Nathalie Le Du, Olivia Swomley, Zoe Maffitt
Production Editor Jessica Rozler
Production Manager Julie Primavera

Workman books are available at special discounts when purchased in bulk for premiums and sales promotions as well as for fund-raising or educational use. Special editions or book excerpts can also be created to specification. For details, contact the Special Sales Director at the address below, or send an email to specialmarkets@workman.com.

Workman Publishing Co., Inc.
225 Varick Street
New York, NY 10014-4381

workman.com
starwars.com
starwarsworkbooks.com

Printed in the United States of America

First printing November 2017

10 9 8 7 6 5 4 3 2 1

WORKBOOKS

This workbook belongs to:

_____

A Place to Climb

489,356 is:

④	⑧	⑨	③	⑤	⑥
Hundred thousands	Ten thousands	Thousands	Hundreds	Tens	Ones

Expanded form shows the place value of each digit in a number.

Expanded form is **400,000 + 80,000 + 9,000 + 300 + 50 + 6**.

Word form is four hundred eighty-nine thousand three hundred fifty-six.

Help Rey and Finn climb the correct routes. Draw lines to match the different forms of each number. (There may be more than one correct route.)

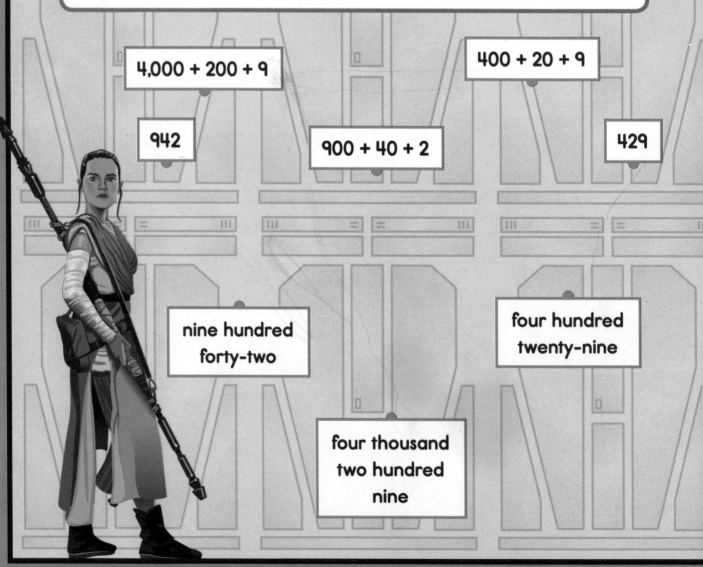

4,000 + 200 + 9

400 + 20 + 9

942

900 + 40 + 2

429

nine hundred forty-two

four hundred twenty-nine

four thousand two hundred nine

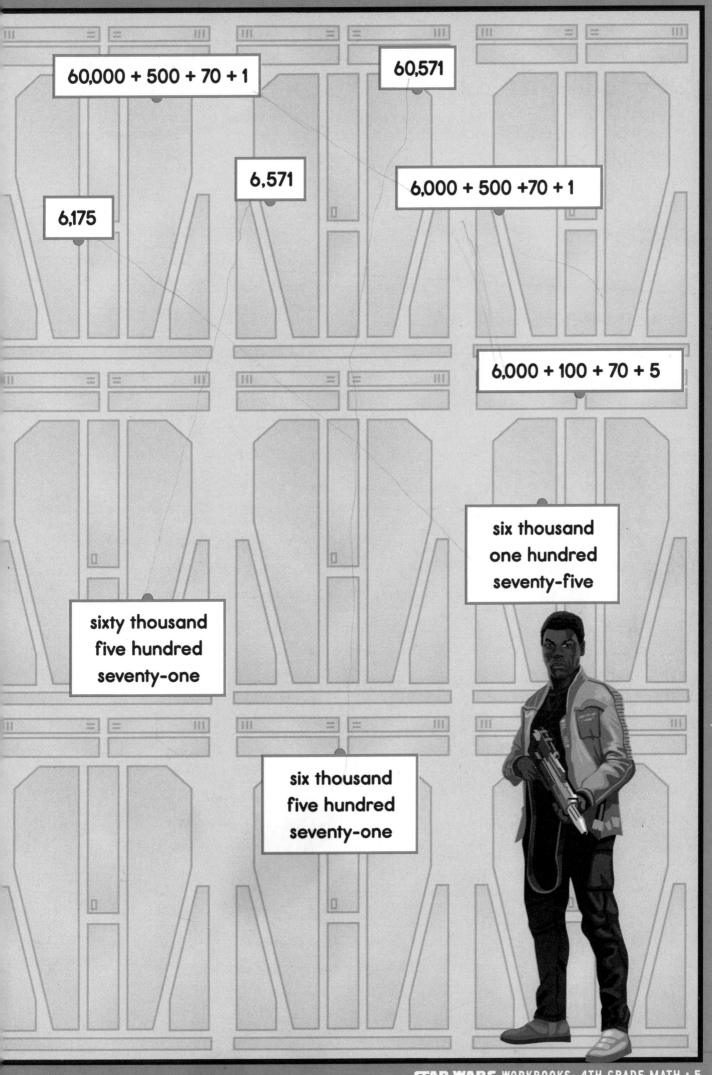

60,000 + 500 + 70 + 1

60,571

6,571

6,000 + 500 +70 + 1

6,175

6,000 + 100 + 70 + 5

six thousand
one hundred
seventy-five

sixty thousand
five hundred
seventy-one

six thousand
five hundred
seventy-one

Multiplication Comparisons

Multiply to solve each **comparison** problem.
Fill in the blanks to find the answer.

If Yoda is about **2** feet tall, and Luke
Skywalker is almost **3** times as tall, about
how tall is Luke?

2 x 3 = ___6___ feet tall

Imagine that a wampa caught **6** ice rats. The
next day, he caught **5** times as many snow
lizards. How many snow lizards did he catch?

6 x _____ **=** _____ snow lizards

There are **27** younglings and **3** Jedi
Masters practicing with their lightsabers.
How many times as many younglings as
Jedi Masters are there?

3 x _____ **= 27**

_____ times as many

Jabba the Hutt is about **4** meters long.
A sandcrawler is about **40** meters long.
How many times longer is the sandcrawler
than Jabba?

_____ x _____ = _____

_____ times longer

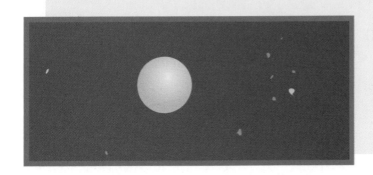

If a moon is populated with about **30** large cities and **10** times as
many smaller cities, about how many small cities are on the moon?

_____ x _____ = _____

_____ smaller cities

Imagine a group of **7** Jedi can lift
7 times as much mass as one
Jedi alone. If one Jedi can lift **80**
kilograms, how many kilograms can
7 Jedi lift?

_____ x _____ = _____

_____ kilograms

Compare and Connect

Luke has **1** lightsaber. The stormtroopers have **4** blaster rifles.

Multiplication comparison:
How many times as many weapons do the stormtroopers have as Luke?

$1 \times ? = 4$
$1 \times 4 = 4$

The stormtroopers have ___4___ times as many weapons.

Addition comparison:
How many more weapons do the stormtroopers have than Luke?

$1 + ? = 4$ or $4 - 1 = ?$
$1 + 3 = 4$ $4 - 1 = 3$

The stormtroopers have ___3___ more weapons than Luke.

Read the example **comparison** problems. Then draw a line from each problem to its equation. (Not all equations will match a problem.)

A handmaiden has **4** different robes. Padmé has **20** times as many robes. How many robes does Padmé have?

$4 + ? = 20$

There were **20** adults and **4** children at a market in Tatooine. How many more adults than children were at the market?

$4 \times 20 = ?$

There are **5** clone troopers outside the Jedi temple. There are **10** times as many battle droids. How many battle droids are there?

5 + ? = 10

There are **5** battle droids approaching from the right and **10** battle droids approaching from the left. How many more droids are approaching from the left?

5 x 10 = ?

5 + 10 = ?

At a Wookiee banquet, **4** guests ate nuts, and **6** times as many guests ate biscuits. How many guests ate biscuits?

10 x 2 = ?

On a mission, **10** stormtroopers climbed a dune, and **2** times as many stormtroopers guarded prisoners. How many stormtroopers guarded prisoners?

4 x 6 = ?

60 – 5 = ?

60 cadets took a stormtrooper exam and **5** failed. How many more cadets passed the exam than failed the exam?

5 x 60 = ?

Spare Part Pairs

Factors are the numbers you multiply to get the product.
You can draw **arrays** to find the factors.

What are the factors of **15**?

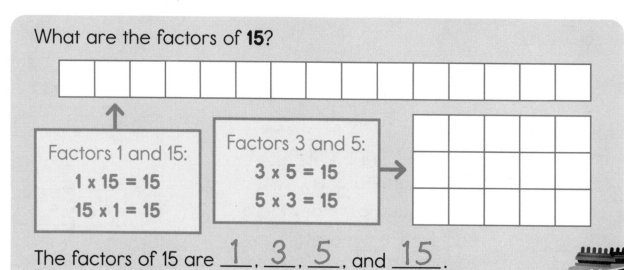

Factors 1 and 15:
1 x 15 = 15
15 x 1 = 15

Factors 3 and 5:
3 x 5 = 15
5 x 3 = 15

The factors of 15 are __1__, __3__, __5__, and __15__.

15 has __4__ different factors.

The droids stacked **12** fuel ports in equal rows and columns.
Fill in the blanks for each array, and then write all the factors of **12**.

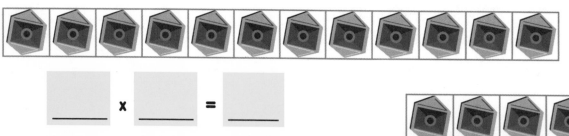

_____ x _____ = _____

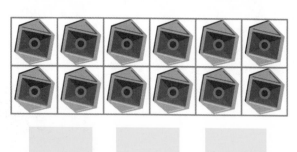

_____ x _____ = _____

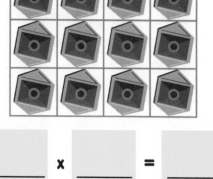

_____ x _____ = _____

The factors of **12** are _____, _____, _____, _____, _____, and _____.

12 has _____ different factors.

There are **5** clone troopers outside the Jedi temple. There are **10** times as many battle droids. How many battle droids are there?

5 + ? = 10

There are **5** battle droids approaching from the right and **10** battle droids approaching from the left. How many more droids are approaching from the left?

5 x 10 = ?

5 + 10 = ?

At a Wookiee banquet, **4** guests ate nuts, and **6** times as many guests ate biscuits. How many guests ate biscuits?

10 x 2 = ?

On a mission, **10** stormtroopers climbed a dune, and **2** times as many stormtroopers guarded prisoners. How many stormtroopers guarded prisoners?

4 x 6 = ?

60 − 5 = ?

60 cadets took a stormtrooper exam and **5** failed. How many more cadets passed the exam than failed the exam?

5 x 60 = ?

Spare Part Pairs

Factors are the numbers you multiply to get the product.
You can draw **arrays** to find the factors.

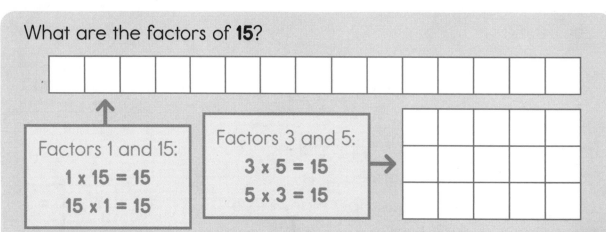

What are the factors of **15**?

Factors 1 and 15:
1 x 15 = 15
15 x 1 = 15

Factors 3 and 5:
3 x 5 = 15
5 x 3 = 15

The factors of 15 are __1__, __3__, __5__, and __15__.

15 has __4__ different factors.

The droids stacked **12** fuel ports in equal rows and columns.
Fill in the blanks for each array, and then write all the factors of **12**.

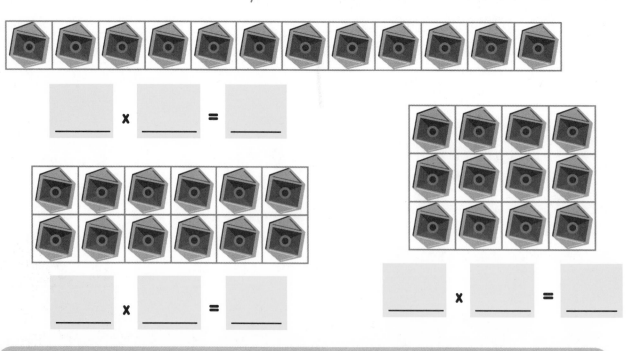

_____ x _____ = _____

_____ x _____ = _____

_____ x _____ = _____

The factors of **12** are _____, _____, _____, _____, _____, and _____.

12 has _____ different factors.

Find all the ways you can help stack **16** access panels by drawing arrays. Write the equation for each array. Then write all the factors of **16**.

$$1 \times 16 = 16$$

The factors of **16** are _____, _____, _____, _____, and _____.

16 has _____ different factors.

Find all the ways you can help stack **13** access panels by drawing arrays. Write the equation for each array. Then write all the factors of **13**.

The factors of **13** are _____ and _____.

13 has _____ different factors.

Prime Territory

A **prime number** has only two factors.
The number **5** is a prime number. Its factors are **1** and **5**.
A **composite number** has three or more factors.
The number **51** is a composite number. Its factors are **1, 3, 17,** and **51**.

Imagine that you have discovered a new planet. Creatures roam over the land and water. The harmless creatures are marked with **prime** numbers. The dangerous creatures are marked with **composite** numbers. Circle the harmless creatures. Cross out the dangerous creatures.

Multiples

Multiples are the products of whole numbers times other whole numbers. A number has a never-ending list of multiples.

Multiples of **3** are **3, 6, 9, 12, 15, 18**…

A bounty hunter stole important supplies, but you found a clue to where they hid their goods.

Planets numbered with a multiple of **4** have hidden starfighter parts. Color these planets **blue**.

Planets numbered with a multiple of **7** have hidden droid parts. Color these planets **pink**.

Planets numbered with a multiple of **10** have hidden food supplies. Color these planets **green**.

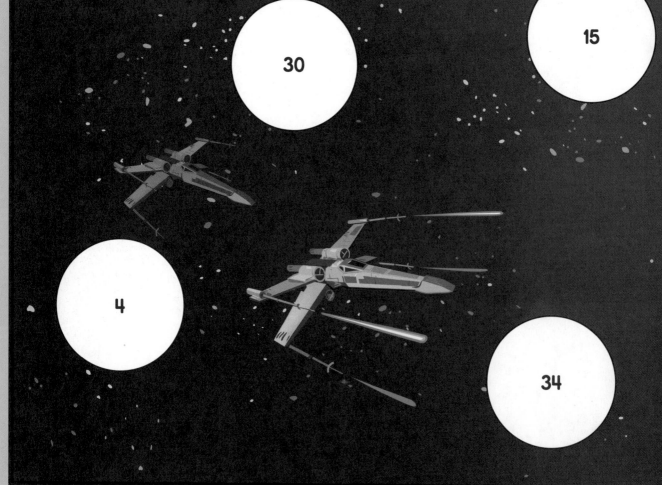

30

15

4

34

Multiples

Multiples are the products of whole numbers times other whole numbers. A number has a never-ending list of multiples.

Multiples of **3** are **3, 6, 9, 12, 15, 18**…

A bounty hunter stole important supplies, but you found a clue to where they hid their goods.

Planets numbered with a multiple of **4** have hidden starfighter parts. Color these planets **blue**.

Planets numbered with a multiple of **7** have hidden droid parts. Color these planets **pink**.

Planets numbered with a multiple of **10** have hidden food supplies. Color these planets **green**.

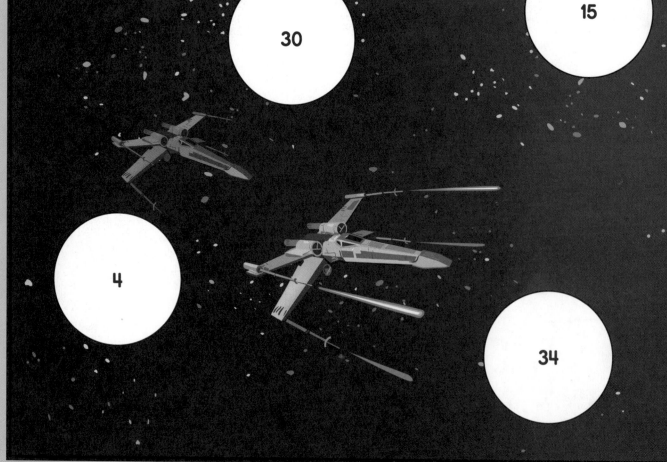

Multiples

Multiples are the products of whole numbers times other whole numbers. A number has a never-ending list of multiples.

Multiples of **3** are **3, 6, 9, 12, 15, 18**...

A bounty hunter stole important supplies, but you found a clue to where they hid their goods.

Planets numbered with a multiple of **4** have hidden starfighter parts. Color these planets **blue**.

Planets numbered with a multiple of **7** have hidden droid parts. Color these planets **pink**.

Planets numbered with a multiple of **10** have hidden food supplies. Color these planets **green**.

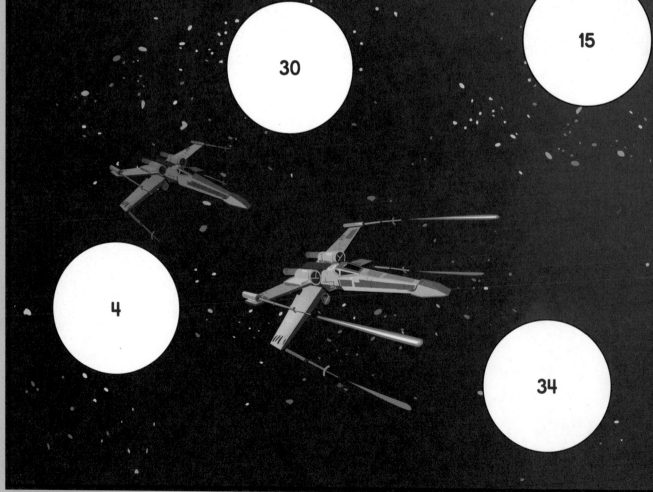

30

15

4

34

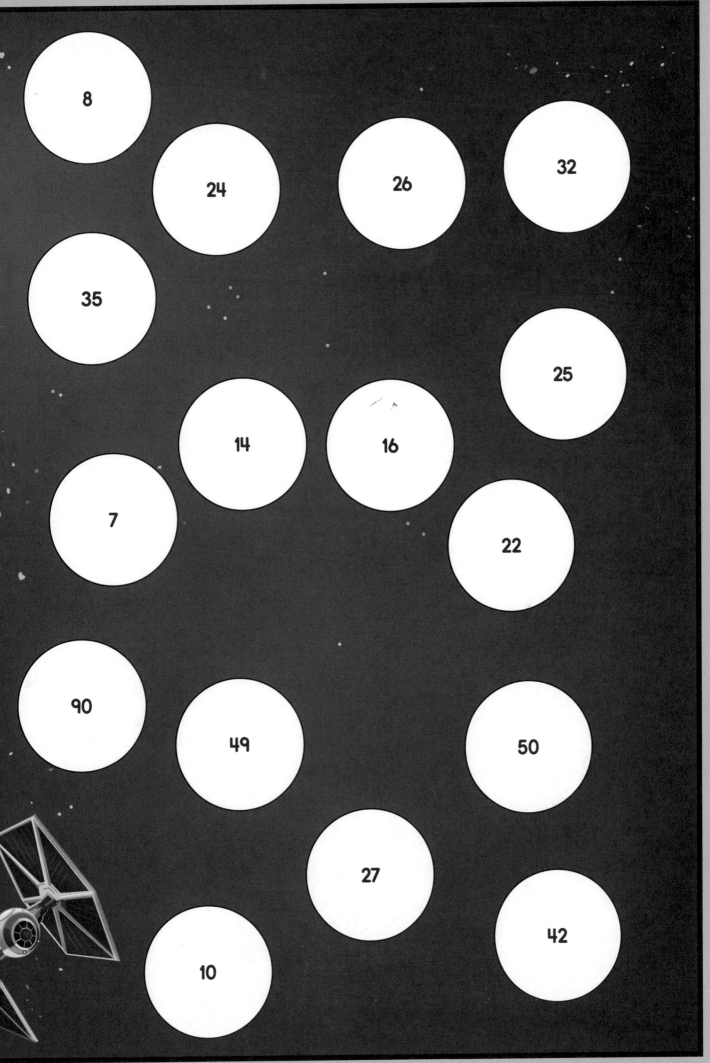

Pattern Progress

Draw each object to continue the **pattern**.
Then fill in the missing numbers in the **number pattern** and **rule**.

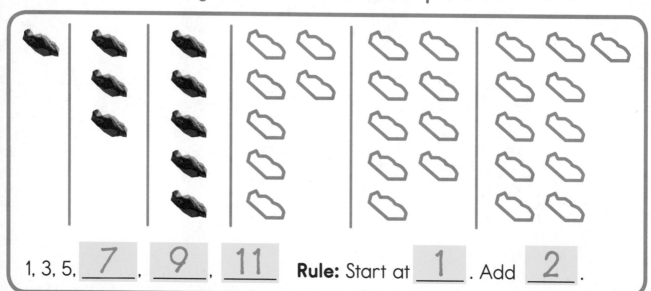

1, 3, 5, __7__, __9__, __11__   **Rule:** Start at __1__ . Add __2__ .

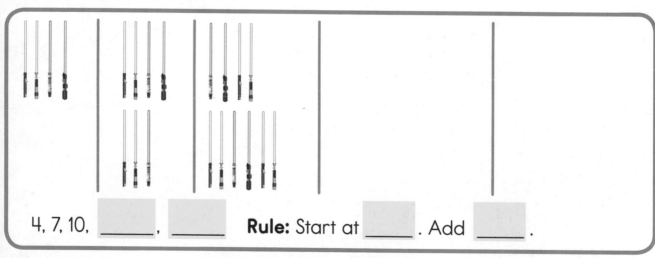

4, 7, 10, _____, _____   **Rule:** Start at _____ . Add _____ .

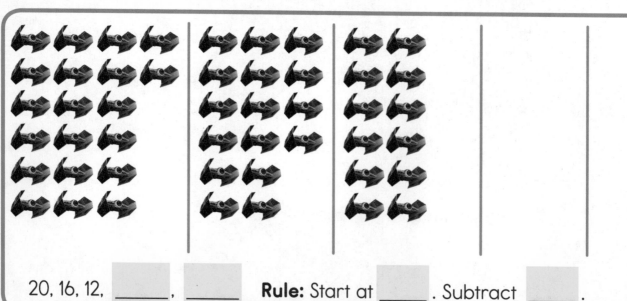

20, 16, 12, _____, _____   **Rule:** Start at _____ . Subtract _____ .

Read the rule below. Then fill in the missing numbers in the number pattern, and draw the missing patterns.

Rule: Start at **15**. Subtract **2**. _____, _____, _____, _____

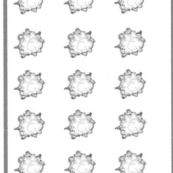

Rule: Start at **15**. Subtract **3**. _____, _____, _____, _____

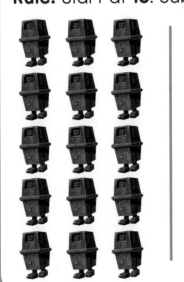

Fill in the blanks with **even** or **odd**.

To make a pattern of only odd numbers, you must begin with an _____ number and add or subtract an _____ number.

To make a pattern that shows only even numbers, you must begin with an _____ number, and add or subtract an _____ number.

Multistep Word Problems

Read each word problem. Complete the steps. Then write the answer.

There were **67** customers at the cantina. Due to long lines, **18** people left. The remaining customers filled booths that sit **7** customers each. How many booths were filled?

Step 1: 67 – 18 = _49_

Step 2: _49_ ÷ _7_ = _7_

_7_ booths

A large pot can hold enough soup to fill **100** bowls at once. There were **235** humans, **71** droids, and **94** aliens who wanted soup. How many pots of soup will the cook have to make?

Step 1: _____

Step 2: _____

_____ pots

A service droid can carry **4** trays of food at a time. Each tray holds **8** plates. If **53** customers order a plate of food, how many plates will the droid have left to carry after the first **4** trays?

Step 1: _____

Step 2: _____

_____ plates

One group of battle droids lines up in **8** rows of **8** droids. Another group lines up in **10** rows of **12** droids. If **97** droids march in the wrong direction, how many droids march in the right direction?

Step 1: _____

Step 2: _____

Step 3: _____ _____ droids

A droid found **153** secret files. She deleted **62** of the files. Then she hid the rest of the files in **7** different computers. How many files were hidden in each computer?

_____ files

Dex's Diner made **196** Devaronian's food cakes, and **20** customers ate **8** food cakes each. The remaining food cakes were put in boxes that hold **6** each. How many boxes were needed for all the remaining cakes?

_____ boxes

Poe Dameron's X-wing is being repaired. If it takes a repair station **3** hours to fix **16** components, how many hours will it take to fix **64** components?

_____ hours

Remember Remainders

When two numbers cannot be divided evenly, the **remainder** is the number left over. Color the tauntauns that have division problems with a remainder of **6**.

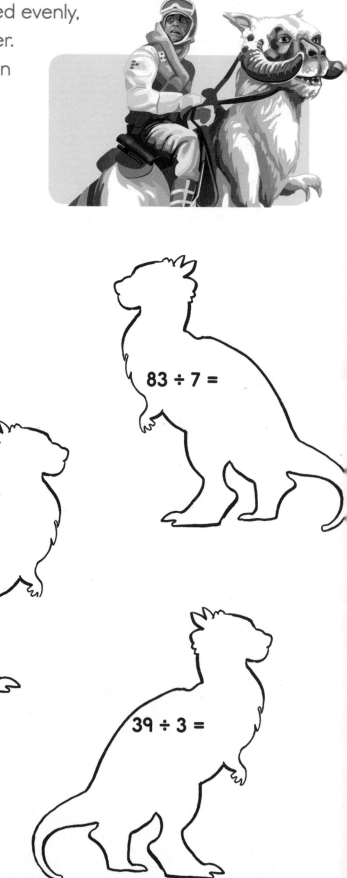

$13 \div 2 = 6$
R1

$83 \div 7 =$

$87 \div 9 =$

$41 \div 7 =$

$39 \div 3 =$

Read each word problem. Then write the answers.

If **38** tauntauns are divided equally into **5** groups for a long journey, how many complete groups are there?

_____ complete groups

How many tauntauns are left over?

_____ tauntauns

If transports can carry only **5** tauntauns each, how many transports are needed to carry all **38** tauntauns at once?

_____ transports

If snowtroopers must transport **50** blasters, and each snowtrooper's backpack can hold **6** blasters, how many backpacks can they fill?

_____ full backpacks

How many extra blasters would be left?

_____ extra blasters

How many snowtroopers will have to go on the mission if all the blasters have to be taken along?

_____ snowtroopers

Millions of Stars

The **place value** of a digit in a number is determined by where it appears in the number. Each place value is **10** times the value of the place to its right, and **100** times the value of the place two places to its right, and so on.

The meaning of **7,777,777** is :

7 x 1,000,000	7 x 100,000	7 x 10,000	7 x 1,000	7 x 100	7 x 10	7
Millions	Hundred thousands	Ten thousands	Thousands	Hundreds	Tens	Ones

Use hyperdrive to jump forward and back along the place value chart to fill in the blanks.

7 x 100 = **700**

7,000 x 10 = _____

7,000 x 100 = _____

7 x 1,000 = _____

77 x 10 = _____

700 ÷ 100 = _____

70,000 ÷ 1,000 = _____

7,000 ÷ 100 = _____

770 ÷ 10 = _____

Multiply or divide on each star.

$300 \times 10 =$ _____

$62 \times 10 =$ _____

$300 \div 10 =$ _____

$417 \times 100 =$ _____

$417,000 \div 10 =$ _____

$62 \times 100 =$ _____

$123,400 \div 100 =$ _____

$1,234 \times 10 =$ _____

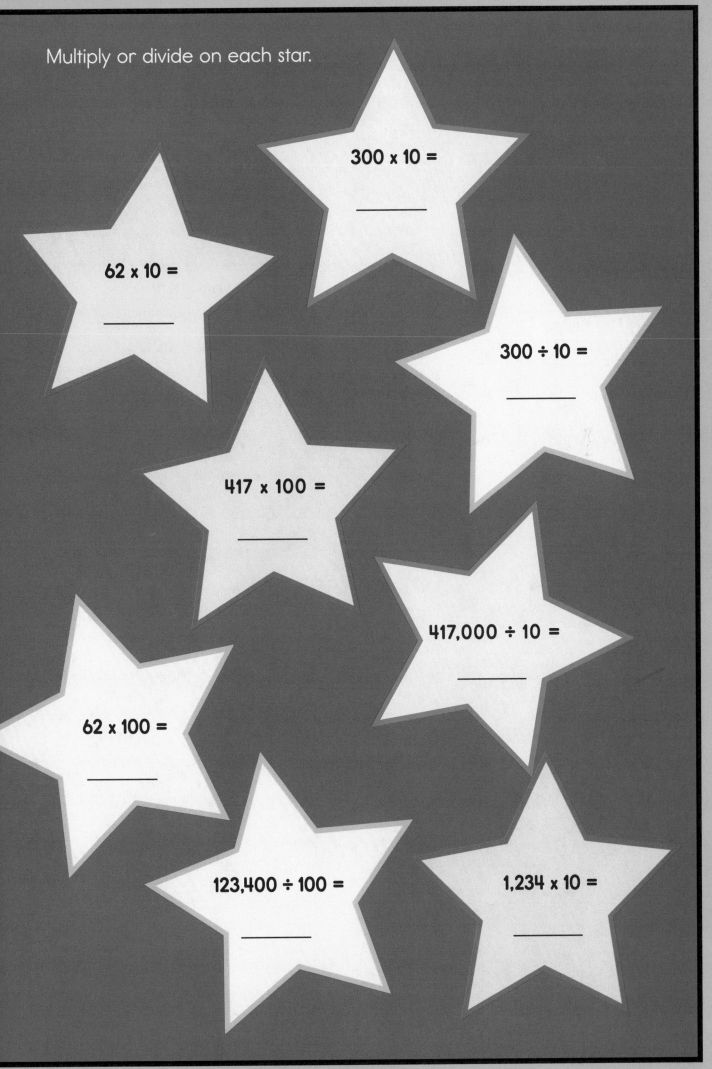

Greater Than or Less Than

Compare the weight of each planet. Begin with the greatest place v[
that is different. Write **<** for **less than** and **>** for **greater than**.

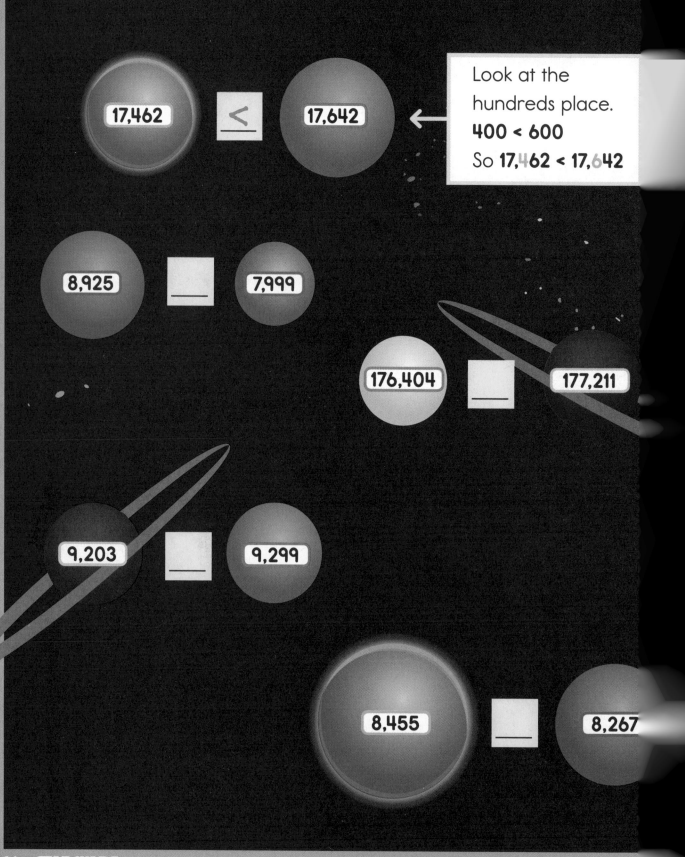

17,462 < 17,642

> Look at the
> hundreds place.
> **400 < 600**
> So **17,462 < 17,642**

8,925 ☐ 7,999

176,404 ☐ 177,211

9,203 ☐ 9,299

8,455 ☐ 8,267

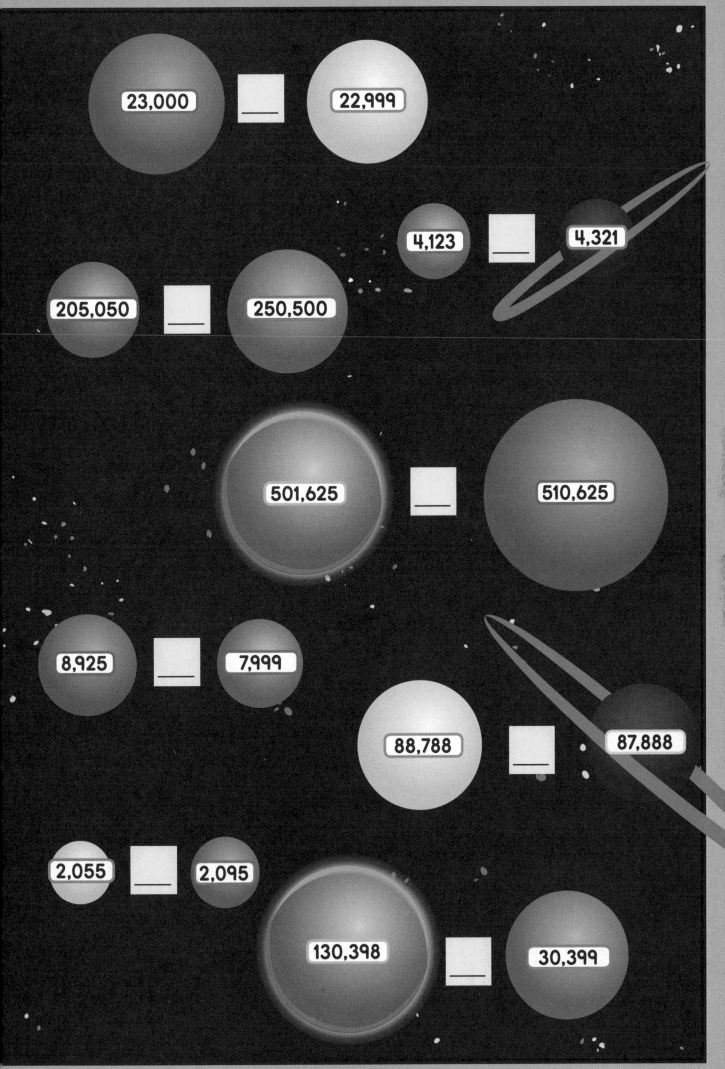

23,000 ___ 22,999

4,123 ___ 4,321

205,050 ___ 250,500

501,625 ___ 510,625

8,925 ___ 7,999

88,788 ___ 87,888

2,055 ___ 2,095

130,398 ___ 30,399

Tic-Tac Rounding

Find the numeral in each place value: If it is 5 or greater round up.
4 or less round down.

11,381,138 rounded to the nearest ten is **11,381,140.**

11,381,138 rounded to the nearest hundred is **11,381,100.**

11,381,138 rounded to the nearest thousand is **11,381,000.**

11,381,138 rounded to the nearest ten thousand is **11,380,000.**

11,381,138 rounded to the nearest hundred thousand is **11,400,000.**

Imagine the Jedi are playing tic-tac-toe to practice their rounding skills. In each grid, help the Jedi round to the place value provided. Draw a line to connect the same numbers and win.

Round to the
nearest ten

9,276 ≈	8,281 ≈	9,272 ≈
_____	_____	_____
19,276 ≈	9,281 ≈	9,288 ≈
_____	_____	_____
10,284 ≈	8,222 ≈	9,275 ≈
_____	_____	_____

Round to the
nearest hundred

52,666 ≈	152,703 ≈	125,703 ≈
_____	_____	_____
126,702 ≈	125,594 ≈	125,672 ≈
_____	_____	_____
126,859 ≈	152,792 ≈	125,749 ≈
_____	_____	_____

104,329 ≈	105,500 ≈	105,129 ≈
_____	_____	_____
103,921 ≈	105,486 ≈	99,129 ≈
_____	_____	_____
105,099 ≈	103,233 ≈	99,536 ≈
_____	_____	_____

Round to the
nearest
thousand

Round to the
nearest ten
thousand

467,815 ≈	63,951 ≈	73,824 ≈
_____	_____	_____
456,315 ≈	463,951 ≈	457,500 ≈
_____	_____	_____
465,315 ≈	443,150 ≈	487,315 ≈
_____	_____	_____

Break Apart and Reassemble

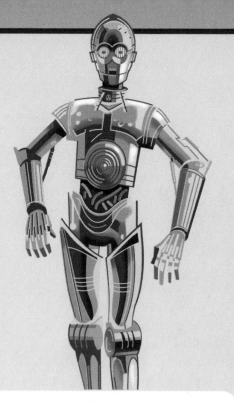

To multiply large numbers, you can **break apart factors** by place value and multiply. Then **reassemble** the numbers by adding them back together to find the final product.

325
x 6

300	+	20	+	5
1,800		120		30

6

1,800
120
+   30

37
x 52

	30	+	7
50	1,500		350
+ 2	60		14

1,500
350
60
+   14

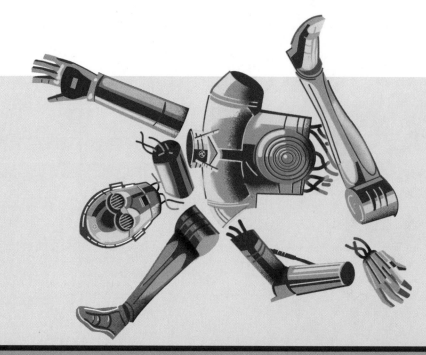

1,223
x 3

	1,000 +	200 +	20 +	3
3	3,000	600	60	9

2,138
x 5

	2,000 +	100 +	30 +	8
5	10,000	500	150	40

48
x 49

	40 +	8
40	1,600	320
+		
9	360	72

91
x 26

	90 +	1
20	1,800	20
+		
6	540	6

15
x 68

	10 +	5
60	600	300
+		
8	80	40

Multiply Large Numbers

Multiply to fill in the blanks. Then add to find the products. Write a complete answer to the question.

Rey finds **18** parts in **1** hour. If she continues at the same rate, how many parts could she find in **24** hours?

18 x 24

	10 +	8
20	20 x 10 = 200	20 x 8 = 160
+		
4	4 x 10 = 40	4 x 8 = 32

```
    200
    160
     40
 +   32
 _____
    432 parts
```

Imagine that you found **33** warehouses of hidden tools. If each warehouse had **99** tools, how many tools are there in all?

33 x 99

	30 +	3
90	90 x 30 = _____	90 x 3 = _____
+		
9	9 x 30 = _____	9 x 3 = _____

+ _____

On Friday, Rey found **26** droid parts. She finds the same number of parts every day for **14** days. How many parts did Rey find in all?

26 x 14

	20	+	6
10	10 x 20 = _____		10 x 6 = _____
+			
4	4 x 20 = _____		4 x 6 = _____

+ _____

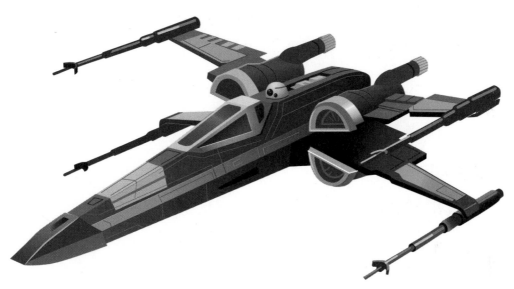

A defect was found in a shipment of X-wing starfighter engines. **1,256** parts will need to be replaced in each one. If **7** X-wing engines need repair, how many parts in all will need to be replaced?

1,256 x 7

	1,000	+	200	+	50	+	6
7	7 x 1,000 =		7 x 200 =				
	_____		_____		_____		_____

+ _____

Ancient Artifacts

Multiply to decode the answer.

27
x 12
_____

J

51
x 34
_____

I

321
x 6
_____

S

175
x 9
_____

C

19
x 42
_____

A

85
x 35
_____

E

66
x 22
_____

D

47
x 18
_____

V

1,212
x   8
_____

H

2,106
x   4
_____

R

Question:

Where do the Jedi keep the oldest and most important texts in the galaxy?

Answer:

	324	2,975	1,452	1,734			
798	8,424	1,575	9,696	1,734	846	2,975	1,926

Battle Droid Break-Apart

To divide large numbers, you can **break apart the dividend** by looking for multiples of the divisor that you subtract from the dividend. Then add the numbers you multiplied by, called **partial quotients**, to find the quotient.

```
                        ? ← quotient
        divisor → 7)854 ← dividend
                   -700   7 x 100 = 700, so subtract 700.
                  ─────         ↑ partial quotient
                    154
                   -140   7 x 20 = 140, so subtract 140.
                  ─────         ↑ partial quotient
                     14
                    -14   7 x 2 = 14, so subtract 14.
                  ─────         ↑ partial quotient
                      0
     100 + 20 + 2 =  122 ← quotient
```

Imagine that the battle droids are in training. Fill in the blanks to find the number of droids in each group. Stragglers will be left behind.

There are **3,698** battle droids. They train in **3** large groups.

```
    3)3,698
     -3,000    3 x 1,000 = 3,000
    ───────
        698

     -_____    3 x 200 = _____
    ───────
         98

     -_____    3 x 30 = _____
    ───────
          8

     -_____    3 x 2 = _____
    ───────
            ← remainder
```

_____ droids in each group

_____ droids left behind

There are **702** battle droids. They train in groups of **6**.

$6\overline{)702}$

6 x 100 = _____

6 x 10 = _____

6 x 7 = _____

_____ droids in each group

_____ droids left behind

There are **2,127** battle droids. They train in groups of **4**.

$4\overline{)2,127}$

4 x _____ = 2,000

4 x _____ = _____

4 x _____ = _____

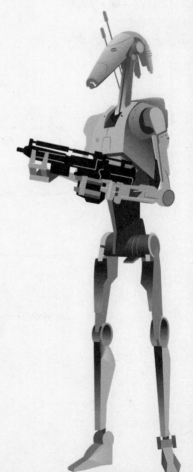

_____ droids in each group

_____ droids left behind

Division Game

Divide each problem. Then color the boxes that have the same remainder with a matching color. To win the game, circle the box without a match.

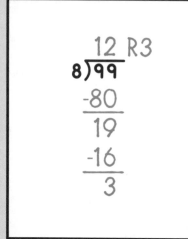

$$8 \overline{)99} \quad \frac{12 \text{ R3}}{}$$
$$\frac{-80}{19}$$
$$\frac{-16}{3}$$

$3 \overline{)299}$

$5 \overline{)174}$

$4 \overline{)761}$

$6 \overline{)737}$

$7 \overline{)181}$

7) 109

3) 3,332

2) 321

8) 1,710

7) 649

Crime Question

Multiply or **divide** to decode the answer.

40
x 40
———

S

2,023
x   3
———

C

4,048
÷   8
———

A

555
÷ 3
———

R

112
x 7
———

I

994
÷ 7
———

L

31
x 29
———

P

1,246
÷   2
———

T

Question:

Where does Jabba the Hutt try to send Luke, Han Solo, and Chewbacca?

Answer:

To the

___ ___ ___ ___ ___ ___ ___
1,600   506   185   142   506   6,069   6,069

___ ___ ___
899   784   623

Kylo's Lightsaber Skills

Imagine that Kylo must **divide** these shapes into equal pieces with his lightsaber. Look at the denominator of the **equivalent fraction**. Then draw lines where Kylo should cut each shape to show the equivalent fraction. Then fill in the missing numerator.

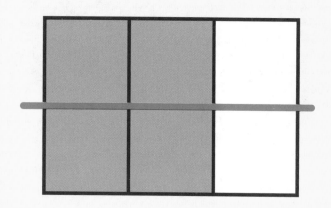

$$\frac{2}{3} = \frac{4}{6}$$

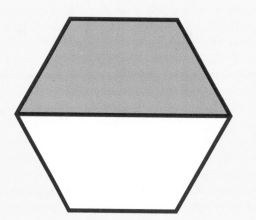

$$\frac{1}{2} = \frac{}{6}$$

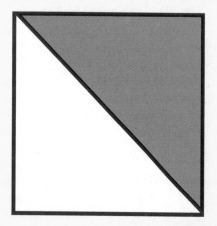

$$\frac{1}{2} = \frac{}{8}$$

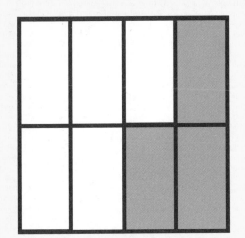

$$\frac{3}{8} = \frac{}{16}$$

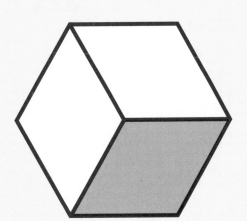

$$\frac{1}{3} = \frac{}{6}$$

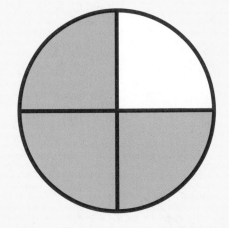

$$\frac{3}{4} = \frac{}{8}$$

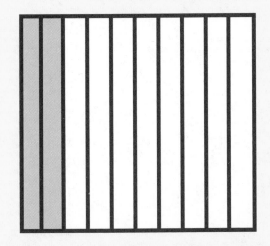

$$\frac{2}{10} = \frac{}{50}$$

Compare to One-Half

The pilots are racing. **Compare** the pilots' distance by using $\frac{1}{2}$ megalight as a benchmark, or point of reference.

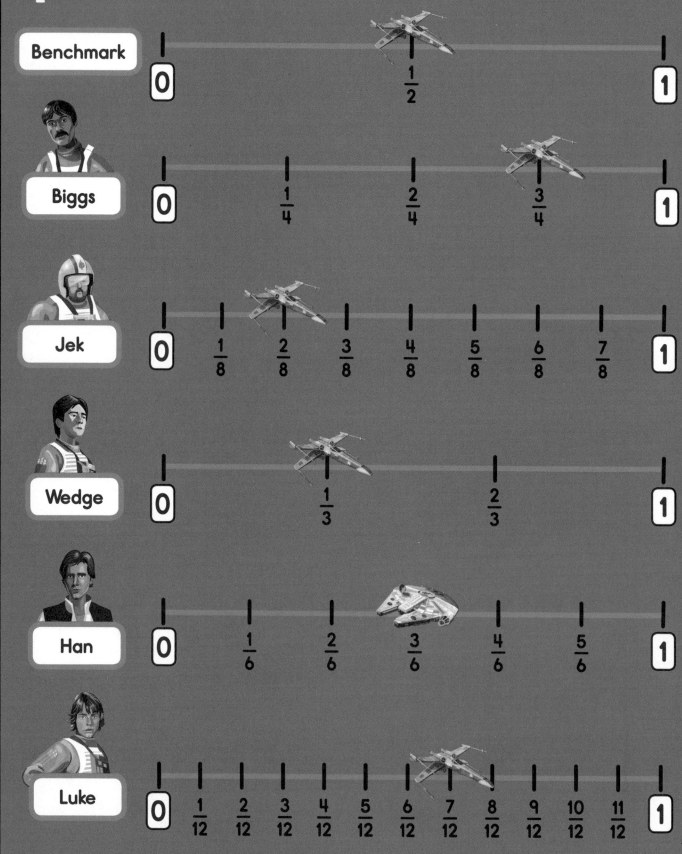

Write the fractions of a megalight for each pilot. Then fill in <, >, or = to compare the distance in two ways.

Biggs and **Jek** $\dfrac{3}{4} > \dfrac{2}{8}$ _____ or $\dfrac{2}{8} < \dfrac{3}{4}$ _____

Wedge and **Han**   _____ or _____

Biggs and **Wedge**   _____ or _____

Luke and **Jek**   _____ or _____

Han and **Luke**   _____ or _____

Wedge and **Luke**   _____ or _____

Biggs and **Han**   _____ or _____

True or False?

Mark the fractions on the appropriate number line and compare. Then write **true** or **false**. If the statement is false, write the correct statement.

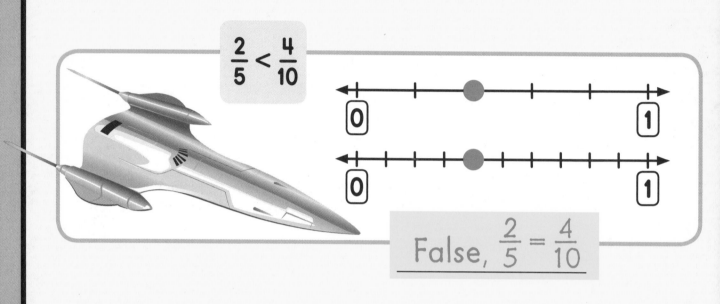

$$\frac{2}{5} < \frac{4}{10}$$

False, $\dfrac{2}{5} = \dfrac{4}{10}$

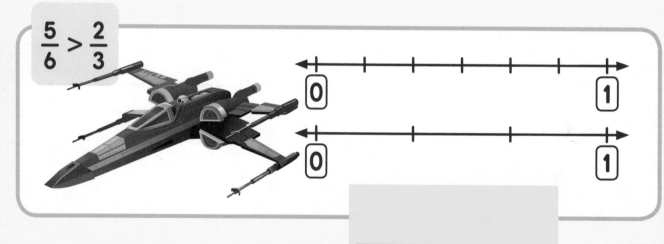

$$\frac{5}{6} > \frac{2}{3}$$

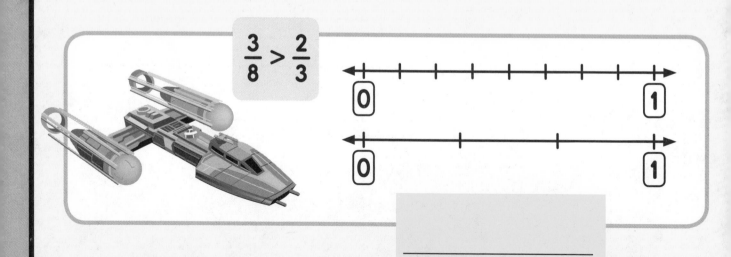

$$\frac{3}{8} > \frac{2}{3}$$

$$\frac{5}{16} > \frac{2}{4}$$

$$\frac{3}{5} < \frac{10}{15}$$

$$\frac{2}{3} > \frac{3}{12}$$

$$\frac{7}{5} < \frac{6}{6}$$

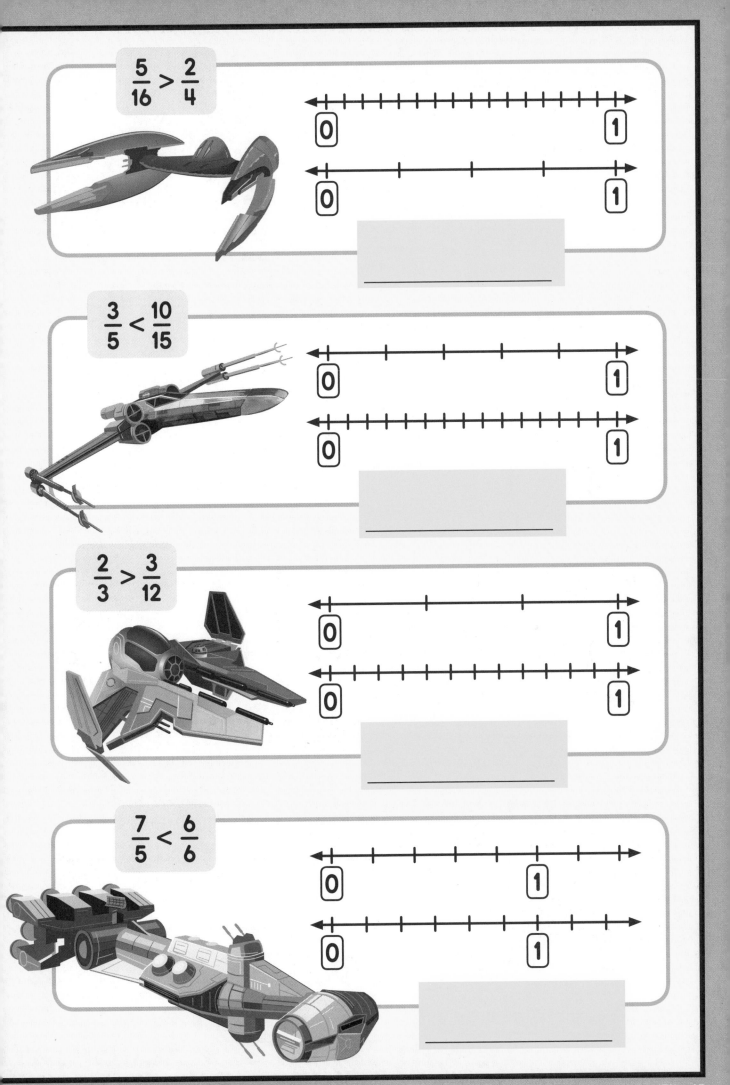

Add and Subtract Fractions

To know how much fuel a fighter has, **add** and **subtract** the fractions.

Adding fractions model

$$\frac{3}{3} + \frac{2}{3} = \frac{5}{3}$$

$\longrightarrow$

0   1   2

Subtracting fractions model

$$\frac{8}{8} - \frac{3}{8} = \frac{5}{8}$$

$\longrightarrow$

0   1

Add and **subtract** fractions by drawing models like the ones above. Then write the answers.

$$\frac{2}{4} + \frac{3}{4} = \frac{}{4}$$

$$\frac{8}{6} - \frac{3}{6} = \frac{}{6}$$

$$\frac{5}{3} - \frac{1}{3} = \frac{}{3}$$

$$\frac{10}{10} - \frac{5}{10} = \frac{}{10}$$

$$\frac{11}{11} - \frac{5}{11} = \frac{}{11}$$

$$\frac{5}{6} + \frac{3}{6} = \underline{\quad}$$

$$\frac{3}{5} + \frac{4}{5} = \underline{\quad}$$

Sum It Up

Fill in each number sentence with a fraction from the screen to make each sum.

$$\frac{2}{8} + \frac{2}{8} + \frac{3}{8} = \frac{7}{8}$$

$$\frac{1}{8} + \frac{1}{8} + \frac{1}{8} + \underline{} = \frac{7}{8}$$

$$\underline{} + \frac{4}{8} + \frac{1}{8} = \frac{7}{8}$$

$$\frac{1}{8} + \underline{} + \frac{1}{8} = \frac{7}{8}$$

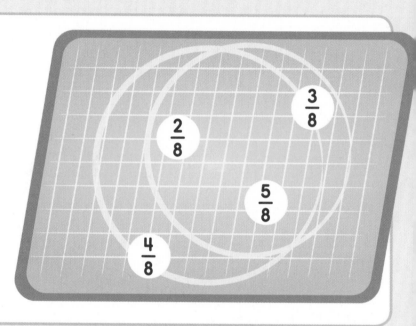

$$\frac{1}{6} + \frac{1}{6} + \underline{} = \frac{6}{6}$$

$$\frac{2}{6} + \frac{2}{6} + \underline{} = \frac{6}{6}$$

$$\underline{} + \frac{2}{6} + \frac{3}{6} = \frac{6}{6}$$

$$\frac{3}{6} + \underline{} + \underline{} + \frac{1}{6} = \frac{6}{6}$$

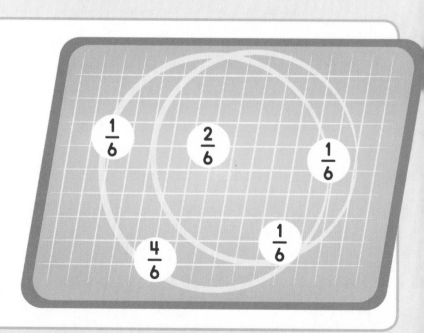

$$\frac{3}{3} + \frac{4}{3} + \underline{\quad} = \frac{9}{3}$$

$$\underline{\quad} + \frac{2}{3} + \frac{2}{3} + \frac{2}{3} = \frac{9}{3}$$

$$\frac{1}{3} + \underline{\quad} + \frac{4}{3} = \frac{9}{3}$$

$$\frac{7}{3} + \underline{\quad} + \underline{\quad} = \frac{9}{3}$$

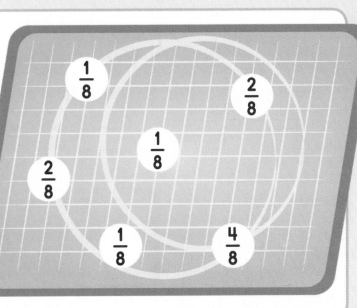

$$\frac{1}{4} + \frac{6}{4} + \underline{\quad} = \frac{11}{4}$$

$$\frac{2}{4} + \underline{\quad} + \frac{6}{4} = \frac{11}{4}$$

$$\frac{7}{4} + \underline{\quad} + \underline{\quad} = \frac{11}{4}$$

$$\underline{\quad} + \underline{\quad} + \frac{1}{4} + \frac{2}{4} = \frac{11}{4}$$

$$\frac{3}{8} + \underline{\quad} + \frac{1}{8} = \frac{8}{8}$$

$$\underline{\quad} + \frac{1}{8} + \frac{5}{8} = \frac{8}{8}$$

$$\frac{1}{8} + \frac{2}{8} + \frac{3}{8} + \underline{\quad} = \frac{8}{8}$$

$$\frac{5}{8} + \underline{\quad} + \underline{\quad} + \underline{\quad} = \frac{8}{8}$$

Mixed Numbers

A **mixed number** has a whole number part and a fraction part.

To **change a mixed number to a fraction**, write the whole number as a fraction, then combine the fractions.

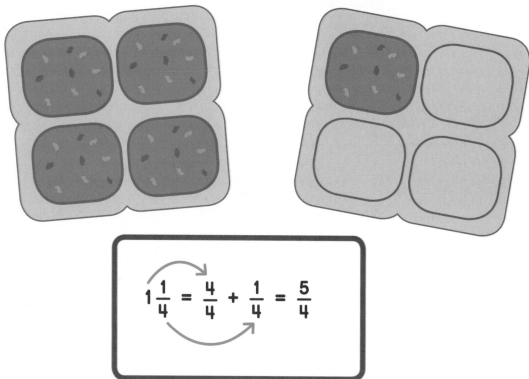

$$1\frac{1}{4} = \frac{4}{4} + \frac{1}{4} = \frac{5}{4}$$

To **change a fraction greater than one to a mixed number**, go in reverse. Break down the fraction into an addition problem. Then write the answer as the mixed number.

$$\frac{5}{4} = \frac{4}{4} + \frac{1}{4} = 1\frac{1}{4}$$

Help Rey calculate the amount of food she earns from Unkar. Fill in the blanks to change the form of these fractions and mixed numbers.

$2\frac{5}{6} =$ _____ + _____ + $\frac{5}{6} = \frac{17}{6}$

$3\frac{7}{8} =$ _____ + _____ + _____ + $\frac{7}{8} =$ _____

$\frac{8}{3} = \frac{3}{3} + \frac{3}{3} +$ _____ = _____

$\frac{9}{2} = \frac{2}{2} + \frac{2}{2} + \frac{2}{2} + \frac{2}{2} +$ _____ = _____

$\frac{11}{6} =$ _____

$2\frac{1}{6} =$ _____

$1\frac{3}{8} =$ _____

$2\frac{6}{8} =$ _____

$\frac{13}{4} =$ _____

$\frac{19}{8} =$ _____

$\frac{7}{6} =$ _____

$3\frac{2}{6} =$ _____

Add Mixed Numbers

To **add mixed numbers with the same denominator,** you can change the mixed numbers to fractions. Add the numerators and keep the denominator.

 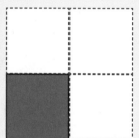 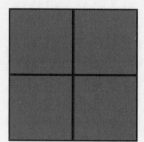 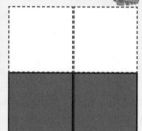

$$1\frac{1}{4} + 1\frac{2}{4} =$$

$$\frac{4}{4} + \frac{1}{4} + \frac{4}{4} + \frac{2}{4} = \frac{4+1+4+2}{4} = \frac{11}{4} \text{ or } 2\frac{3}{4}$$

You can also add the whole numbers, and then add the fractions.

$$1\frac{1}{4} + 1\frac{2}{4} = 2 + \frac{3}{4} = 2\frac{3}{4}$$

The Ewoks are counting their arrows. Some quivers are full, while others are only partially full, so fractions are used. Write the **sum** on each Ewok quiver.

$1\frac{2}{3} + \frac{2}{3} =$

$2\frac{2}{8} + 2\frac{5}{8} =$

$1\frac{3}{4} + 2\frac{1}{4} =$

$1\frac{2}{6} + 4\frac{4}{6} + \frac{5}{6} =$

$1\frac{2}{5} + \frac{4}{5} =$

$1\frac{2}{10} + \frac{4}{10} + 1\frac{7}{10} =$

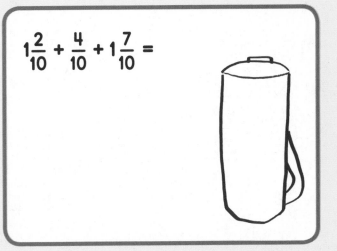

Subtract Mixed Numbers

To **subtract mixed numbers with the same denominator**, you can change the mixed numbers to fractions. Subtract the numerators and keep the denominator.

$$3\frac{4}{6} - 1\frac{2}{6} = \frac{22}{6} - \frac{8}{6} = \frac{14}{6} = 2\frac{2}{6}$$

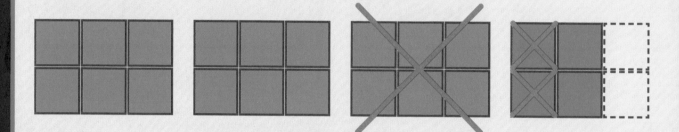

You can also subtract the whole numbers, and then subtract the fractions.

Write the difference on each Ewok quiver.

$$3\frac{5}{8} - 1\frac{1}{8} =$$

$2\dfrac{1}{3} - \dfrac{2}{3} =$

$2\dfrac{4}{6} - 2\dfrac{1}{6} =$

$6 - 2\dfrac{1}{6} =$

$2\dfrac{2}{5} - 1\dfrac{3}{5} =$

$3\dfrac{5}{6} - 1\dfrac{4}{6} =$

$2\dfrac{1}{4} - 1\dfrac{3}{4} =$

$1\dfrac{11}{12} - 1\dfrac{1}{12} =$

Fraction Word Problems

Solve each problem.

If Luke trained with Yoda for $2\frac{1}{3}$ hours in the morning and $2\frac{2}{3}$ hours in the afternoon, how many hours did Luke train that day?

_____ hours

If Luke transported $29\frac{7}{8}$ gallons of water through the jungle, and he drank $9\frac{5}{8}$ gallons, how much water did he have left?

_____ gallons

If Luke hiked for $10\frac{1}{4}$ miles, and then hiked $8\frac{3}{4}$ miles more, how far did Luke hike in all?

_____ miles

Imagine that the swamp trees on the planet Dagobah grow very quickly. A tree that was $3\frac{3}{4}$ meters tall one week grew to $9\frac{3}{4}$ meters tall the next week. How much did the tree grow in one week?

_____ meters

Yoda had **7** lessons to teach Luke. He taught $3\frac{1}{2}$ of them before Luke interrupted. How many more lessons did Yoda still need to teach?

_____ lessons

Imagine that Luke jumped $10\frac{2}{5}$ meters forward on his first try. Then he jumped $18\frac{2}{5}$ meters forward on his second try. How many meters did he jump in all?

_____ meters

If Luke has $26\frac{2}{3}$ pounds of food in his X-wing, and Yoda has $22\frac{2}{3}$ pounds of food hanging from a vine, how much food do they have all together?

_____ pounds

Imagine that Yoda lifted $10\frac{3}{8}$ pounds of stones and $11\frac{7}{8}$ pounds of X-wing parts with the Force. How many pounds did he lift in total?

_____ pounds

Multiply Fraction Credits

Jabba the Hutt has **5** coins worth $\frac{1}{2}$ credit each.

Together they are worth $5 \times \frac{1}{2} = \frac{5}{2}$ or $2\frac{1}{2}$

Draw lines to match the credits that have the same value.

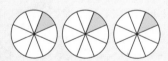   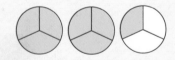

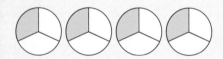

   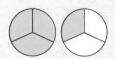

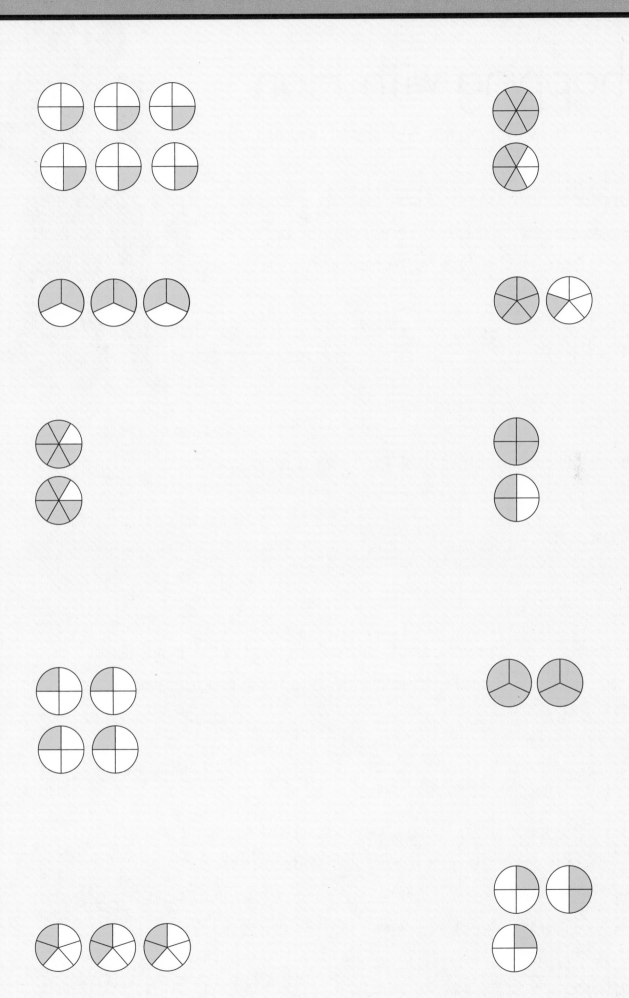

Shopping with Han

Read each word problem. Multiply to find the answer.

Imagine that Han has **3** coins worth $\frac{1}{3}$ credit each. He wants to buy a light freighter part that costs **1** credit. Does he have enough?

$3 \times \frac{1}{3} = \frac{3 \times 1}{3} = \frac{3}{3} = 1$ <u>Yes! He has 1 credit.</u>

If Han buys Chewie a bowcaster with **20** coins worth $\frac{1}{4}$ credit each, what was the cost of the bowcaster?

$20 \times \frac{1}{4} =$

_____ credits

Imagine that Chewie needs quarrels to load in the bowcaster. Each projectile costs $\frac{2}{6}$ credit. How much will **6** quarrels cost?

$6 \times \frac{2}{6} =$

_____ credits

Chewie also needs new power packs to fix his bowcaster, and some others that are broken. Han buys **9** power packs at $\frac{1}{2}$ credit each. How much will he pay for all 9 power packs?

$9 \times \frac{1}{2} =$

_____ credits

Fill in the blanks to answer the questions.

Imagine that Han would like to buy a large robe or cloak for a disguise.

He has **30** coins worth $\frac{5}{6}$ credits each. Which of the robes shown below can he buy?

Camouflage Cloak
$30 \frac{5}{6}$ credits

All-Temperature Cloak
100 credits

Dark Cloak
25 credits

$30 \times \frac{5}{6} =$

Han can buy the _____

because he has _____ credits.

Han is an expert at fixing starships. Imagine that he sees a new welding torch that will help him weld pieces of metal together. He has **15** coins worth $\frac{3}{8}$ credit each. The welding torch costs **6** credits. Does Han have enough to buy the welding torch?

Explain your answer.

$15 \times \frac{3}{8} =$

_____

More Fraction Word Problems

Read each word problem. Write the equation in the space. Then write the answer in the yellow box.

On the planet Hoth, **52** inches of snow fell in 1 day. The next day $\frac{1}{4}$ of that amount of snow fell. How much snow fell the second day?

_____ **inches**

If a fully charged battery on a droid will last for **10** weeks, how long will the battery work if it is only $\frac{3}{5}$ charged?

$$10 \times \frac{3}{5} = \frac{30}{5} = 6$$

_____ **weeks**

Imagine that at full strength, a stormtrooper can jump **9** feet high. He is now at $\frac{3}{4}$ of his full power. How high can he jump?

_____ **feet**

A medical assistant droid stacks **20** boxes of medicine one on top of the other. Each box is $\frac{1}{3}$ of a meter tall. How tall is the stack of boxes?

_____ **meters**

The Modal Nodes play **16** songs every hour at the cantina. How many songs will they play in $\frac{2}{3}$ of an hour?

_____ **songs**

Astromech droids can fix **4** starships in **1** hour. How many starships can they fix in $\frac{5}{6}$ of an hour?

_____ **starships**

Imagine that Leia has a piece of rope **18** feet long. She cuts off $\frac{3}{8}$ of its length and uses the rest for an escape. How many feet of rope did she cut off?

_____ **feet**

Tic-Tac Tenths and Hundredths

Fractions with a denominator of **10** can be written as an equivalent fraction with a denominator of **100**.

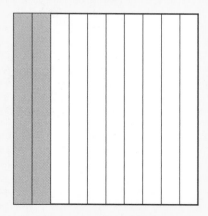

$$\frac{2}{10} = \frac{20}{100}$$

$$\frac{2}{10} = \frac{2 \times 10}{10 \times 10} = \frac{20}{100}$$

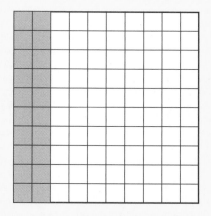

Multiply the numerator and denominator by **10** to write each tenth as an equivalent fraction in hundredths. Color the grid to show that they equal the same amount.

$\frac{5}{10} =$

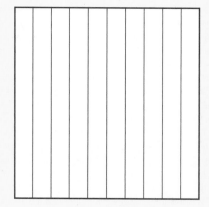 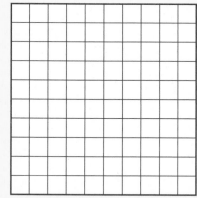

$\frac{7}{10} =$

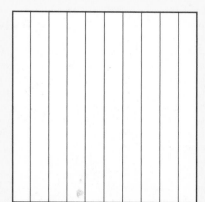 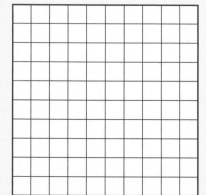

To add tenths and hundredths, express the tenths as an equivalent fraction in hundredths.

$$\frac{3}{10} + \frac{22}{100} = \frac{30}{100} + \frac{22}{100} = \frac{52}{100}$$

Add the fractions. Then, help Bossk and 4-LOM hunt for sums that are the same. Draw a line through three in a row.

$\frac{1}{10} + \frac{43}{100}$	$\frac{43}{10} + \frac{1}{10}$	$\frac{4}{10} + \frac{31}{100}$
$\frac{13}{100} + \frac{4}{10}$	$\frac{5}{10} + \frac{23}{100}$	$\frac{3}{10} + \frac{5}{100}$
$\frac{3}{10} + \frac{23}{100}$	$\frac{23}{100} + \frac{4}{10}$	$\frac{3}{100} + \frac{23}{100}$

$\frac{1}{10} + \frac{57}{100}$	$\frac{25}{100} + \frac{5}{10}$	$\frac{5}{10} + \frac{70}{100}$
$\frac{25}{100} + \frac{3}{10}$	$\frac{6}{10} + \frac{15}{100}$	$\frac{5}{10} + \frac{7}{100}$
$\frac{5}{10} + \frac{60}{100}$	$\frac{7}{10} + \frac{5}{100}$	$\frac{25}{100} + \frac{35}{100}$

Decimal Fractions

You can write fractions as decimals.

	ONES		TENTHS	HUNDREDTHS	
$\frac{1}{10}$ =	0	.	1	0 =	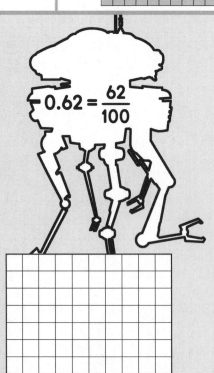
$\frac{1}{100}$ =	0	.	0	1 =	
$\frac{101}{100}$ =	1	.	0	1 =	

Color the grid to show **0.62**.

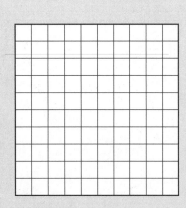

$0.62 = \frac{62}{100}$

Color the grids to show **1.25**.

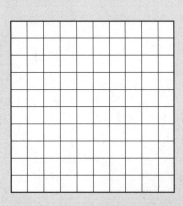

$1.25 = \frac{125}{100}$

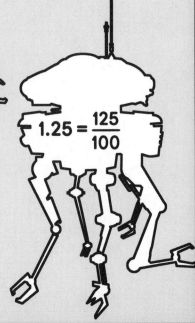

Pick Probe Droids

Match the equivalent fractions and decimals on the probe droids.
Color the probe droids that have the same value with the same color.

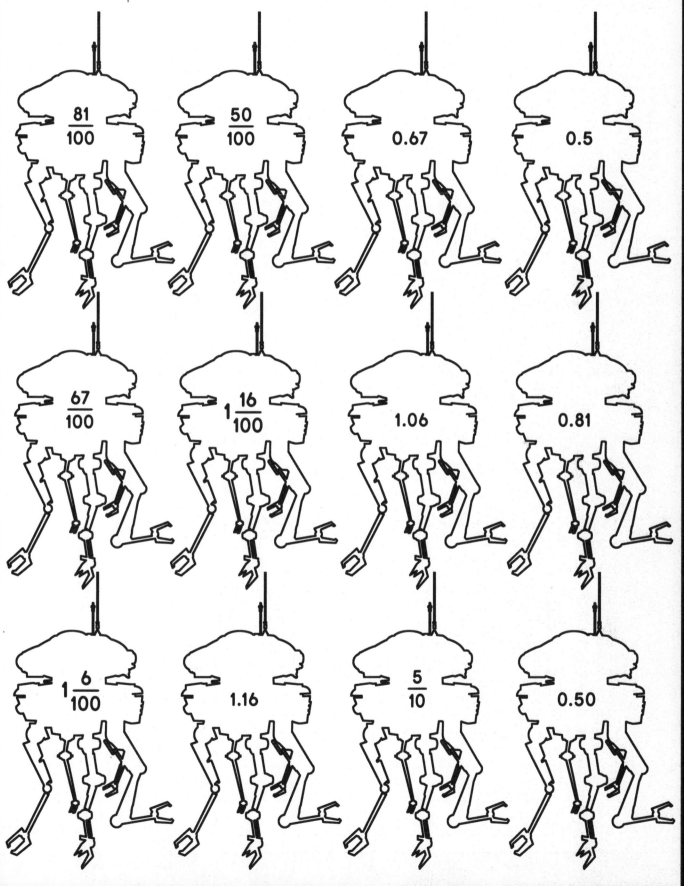

$\dfrac{81}{100}$ $\dfrac{50}{100}$ 0.67   0.5

$\dfrac{67}{100}$ $1\dfrac{16}{100}$ 1.06   0.81

$1\dfrac{6}{100}$ 1.16 $\dfrac{5}{10}$ 0.50

Compare Decimals

The Jawas disagree about which decimal is greater. Show them by writing <, > or =.

Compare by tenths.

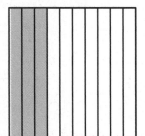

 0.3 < 0.7

Compare by hundredths.

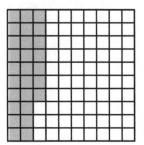 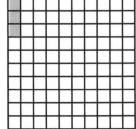

○

Compare tenths and hundredths by making tenths into hundredths.

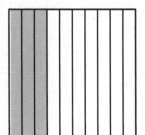 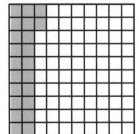

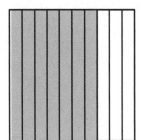 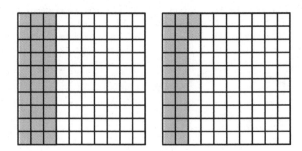

 ○

 ○

0.6 ◯ 0.2

0.90 ◯ 0.9

0.09 ◯ 0.02

0.46 ◯ 0.64

0.35 ◯ 0.15

0.66 ◯ 0.9

0.7 ◯ 0.77

0.1 ◯ 0.11

0.47 ◯ 0.7

0.4 ◯ 0.9

0.9 ◯ 0.89

0.8 ◯ 0.80

0.3 ◯ 0.53

0.1 ◯ 0.01

Colorful Decimal Fractions

Imagine that C-3PO is working on a new circuit board. Use **four** different colors to color the **hundredths** circuit board any way you wish.

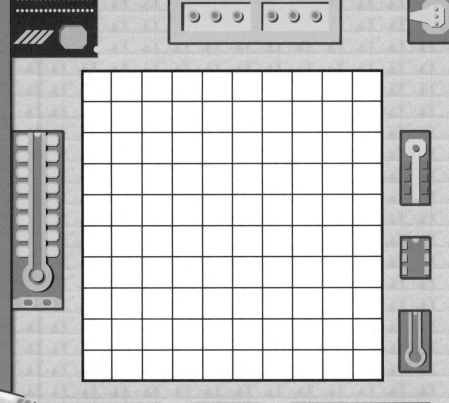

Each color represents a different hundredths decimal. Fill in the key to show what decimal each color represents.

Color 1: ___yellow___ = Decimal 0.32

Color 2: _____ = Decimal _____

Color 3: _____ = Decimal _____

Color 4: _____ = Decimal _____

Write the decimals in order from least to greatest.

_____, _____, _____, _____

Use **five** different colors to color another hundredths circuit board any way you wish.

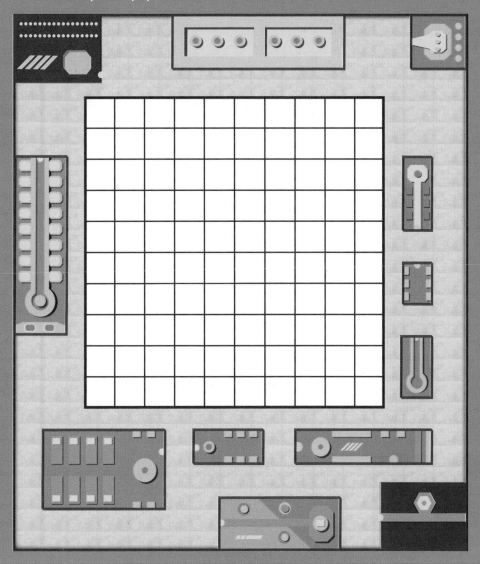

Each color represents a different hundredths decimal. Fill in the key to show what decimal each color represents.

Color 1: _____ = Decimal _____

Color 2: _____ = Decimal _____

Color 3: _____ = Decimal _____

Color 4: _____ = Decimal _____

Color 5: _____ = Decimal _____

Write the decimals in order from greatest to least.

_____, _____, _____, _____, _____

Area and Perimeter Formulas

The **area** of a rectangle is the number of square units that cover a region. Area is measured in square units.

Area = Length x Width
A = L x W

The **perimeter** of a rectangle is the total length of its sides.

Perimeter = Length + Width + Length + Width
P = L + W + L + W
P = (2 x L) + (2 x W)
P = 2 x (L + W)

Fill in the blanks in the formulas to find each answer.

Imagine that the clone troopers have stormed aboard a captured ship. What is the **area** of the cargo hold that they must search?

A = _____ x _____ = _____ square feet

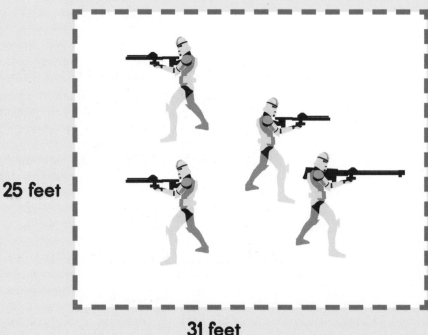

25 feet

31 feet

? meters

9 meters

Imagine that the **area** of the clone troopers' weapon room is **162 square meters.** What is the **length** of the missing side of the room?

A = L x _____ = _____

A = _____ x _____ = _____

L = _____ meters

Imagine that Jango is watching a clone cadet squad during training. What is the **perimeter** of the **square** bay they are gathered in?

P = _____ + _____ + _____ + _____

P = _____ meters

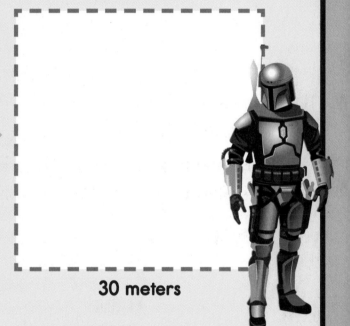

30 meters

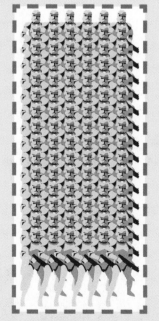

? meters

4 meters

Imagine that the clone troopers are in a training formation, and the **area** of their formation is **36 meters.** What is the **length** of their formation?

A = L x _____ = _____

A = _____ x _____ = _____

L = _____ meters

Rebel Surprises

Use **area** and **perimeter** formulas with length (**l**) and width (**w**) to find the missing dimension. Then use the key to color the rebel targets.

$l = 3$

$w = 2$

$P =$ _____

$l = 10$

$w = 5$

$P =$ _____

$l = 21$

$w = 8\frac{1}{2}$

$P =$ _____

$l = 15$

$w = 2$

$A =$ _____

$P = 14$

$w = 3$

$l =$ _____

$l = 6\frac{1}{2}$

$w = 2$

A = _____

$l = 20$

$w = \frac{1}{2}$

A = _____

Key:

5 = ◻

9 = ◻

30 = ◻

10 = ◻

$l = 7$

$w = 6$

A = _____

$l = 8$

$w = \frac{5}{8}$

A = _____

$l = 12$

$w = 9$

P = _____

P = 15

$w = 2\frac{1}{2}$

$l = $ _____

P = 24

$w = 3$

$l = $ _____

Meteorites on Endor

Imagine that the Ewoks have just found the remains of a meteor shower on Endor. They have picked up the following meteorites:

A meteorite $4\frac{1}{4}$ cm long.

A meteorite $5\frac{1}{4}$ cm long.

A meteorite **5** cm long.

A meteorite $5\frac{1}{4}$ cm long.

A meteorite $4\frac{1}{4}$ cm long.

A meteorite $4\frac{3}{4}$ cm long.

The **line plot** below shows the data from a meteor shower the year before. Draw Xs to include this year's data on the line plot.

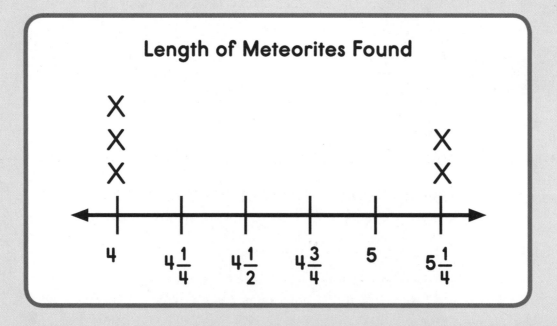

Length of Meteorites Found

Fill in the blanks using data from the line plot.

How many meteorites were found in all? _____

The longest meteorite found was _____ centimeters.

The shortest meteorite was _____ centimeters shorter than
the longest meteorite.

An Ewok finds a new meteorite $6\frac{3}{4}$ centimeters long. How much
longer is that than the longest meteorite found so far?

_____ centimeters

Another Ewok finds a new meteorite $1\frac{3}{4}$ centimeters longer than
the shortest meteorite length on the line plot. How long is it?

_____ centimeters

The new meteorites will change the line plot. What numbers do
you have to add to the scale at the bottom of the line plot?

_____

Angles

ray

angle

ray

An **angle** is formed by two **rays** that share an endpoint.

It is measured by the amount a ray turns through a circle.

A **circle** has **360 degrees**. **1 degree** = $\frac{1}{360}$ of a circle.

Luke is scanning space for incoming fighters. How many **degrees** has he scanned?

Luke turned $\frac{1}{4}$ of a circle.

$\frac{1}{4}$ x 360 degrees = $\frac{360}{4}$ = _____ degrees

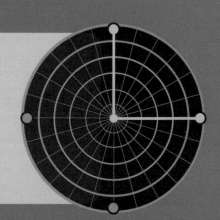

Luke turned $\frac{1}{2}$ of a circle.

$\frac{1}{2}$ x 360 degrees = $\frac{360}{2}$ = _____ degrees

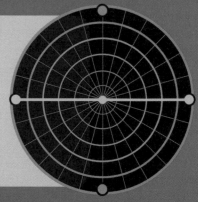

Luke turned $\frac{1}{3}$ of a circle.

$\frac{1}{3}$ x 360 degrees = $\frac{360}{3}$ = _____ degrees

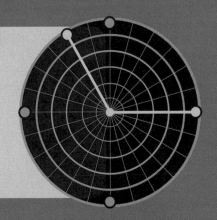

Luke turned $\frac{1}{5}$ of a circle.

$\frac{1}{5}$ x 360 degrees = _____ degrees

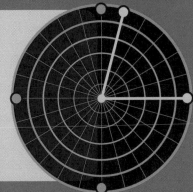

Luke turned $\frac{1}{6}$ of a circle.

$\frac{1}{6}$ x 360 degrees = _____ degrees

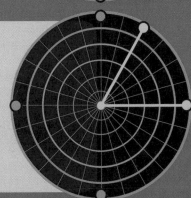

Luke turned $\frac{1}{10}$ of a circle.

$\frac{1}{10}$ x 360 degrees = _____ degrees

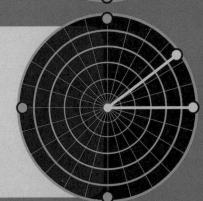

Luke turned $\frac{1}{8}$ of a circle.

$\frac{1}{8}$ x 360 degrees = _____ degrees

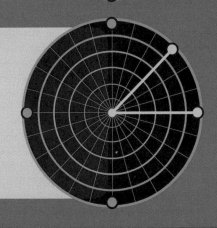

Measure Angles

You can use a **protractor** to measure angles.

If the angle opens from the right, use the bottom scale.

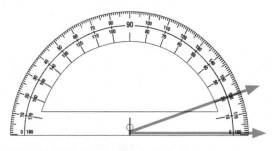

20 degrees (20°)

If the angle opens from the left, use the top scale.

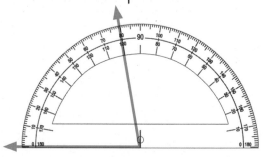

80 degrees (80°)

Write the degree of each angle.

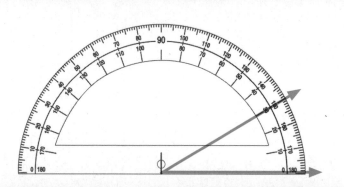

_____ degrees

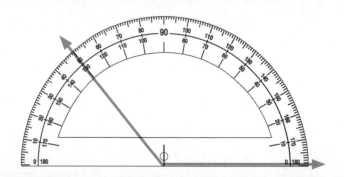

_____ degrees

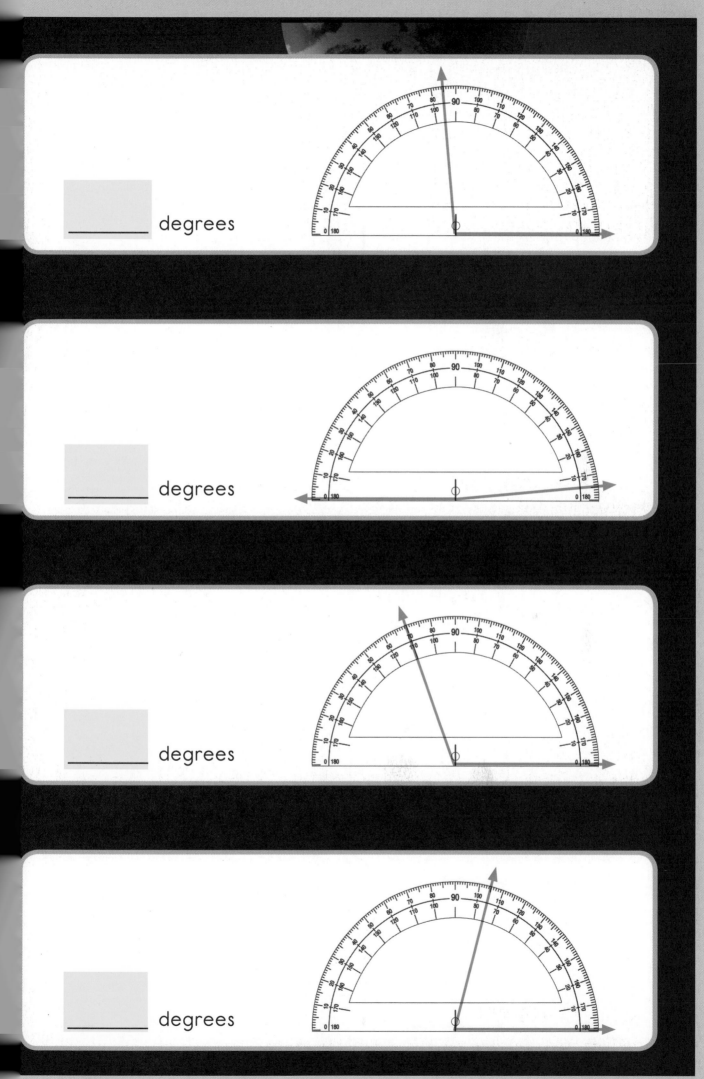

_____ degrees

_____ degrees

_____ degrees

_____ degrees

Code with Angles

Add to find a **missing angle**.

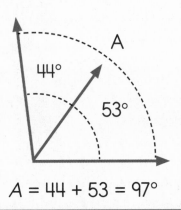

$A = 44 + 53 = 97°$

Subtract to find a **missing angle**.

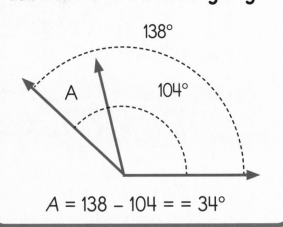

$A = 138 - 104 = = 34°$

Add or subtract to find a missing angle. Use your solutions to answer the question.

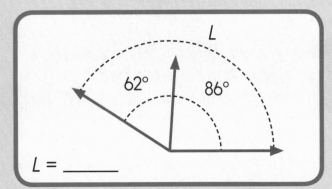

$L =$ _____

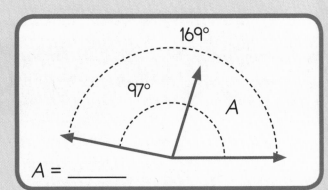

$A =$ _____

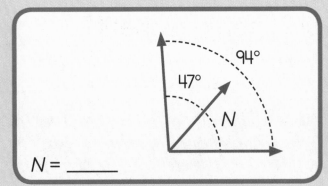

$N =$ _____

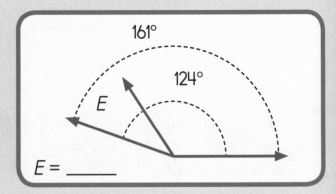

$E =$ _____

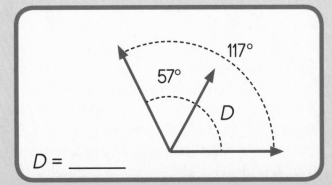

$D =$ _____

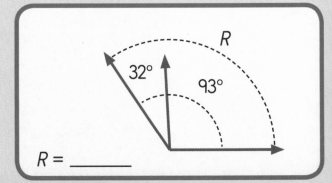

$R =$ _____

Question:

What was Princess Leia's home planet?

Answer:

—   —   —   —   —   —   —   —

72   148   60   37   125   72   72   47

The Language of Geometry

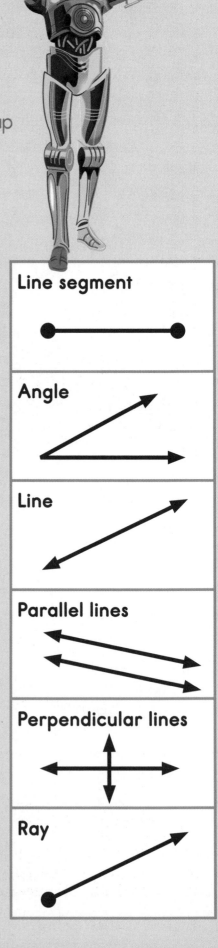

C-3PO knows many languages—including the language of geometry. Help him fix the mixed-up messages below. **Draw lines** to match each message with a shape.

I go on and on in both directions.	Line segment 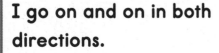
I am made up of 2 rays that meet in a point.	Angle
I have 2 endpoints.	Line
I am 2 lines that never meet.	Parallel lines
I have 1 endpoint and my other side goes on forever.	Perpendicular lines
I am 2 lines that meet to make square corners.	Ray

Use the key to color in the lightsabers.

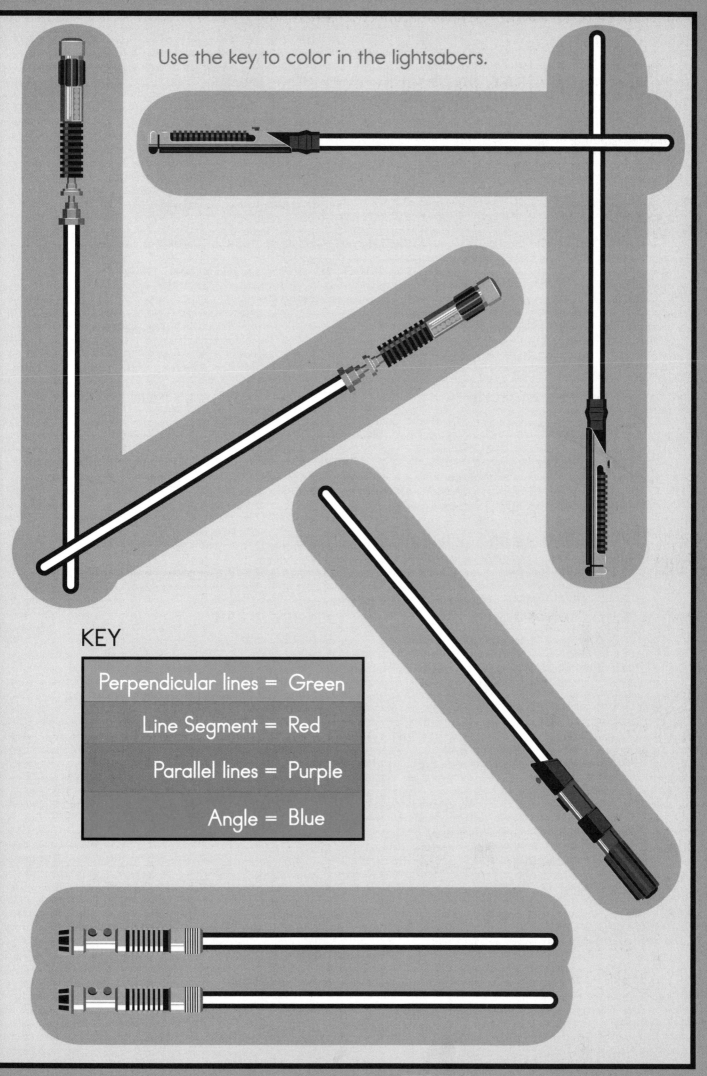

KEY

Perpendicular lines = Green

Line Segment = Red

Parallel lines = Purple

Angle = Blue

More About Angles

A **right angle** measures exactly **90°**.

An **acute angle** is **less than 90°**.

An **obtuse angle** is **greater than 90°**.

right

acute

obtuse

Imagine that rebel squadrons must land on certain shapes.

Green Squadron pilots can land on shapes with all obtuse angles.

Blue Squadron pilots can land on shapes with exactly 2 right angles and at least 1 acute and 1 obtuse angle.

Gold Squadron pilots can land on shapes with exactly 2 pairs of parallel sides and no right angles.

Yellow Squadron pilots can land on shapes with all acute angles.

Red Squadron pilots can land on shapes with parallel and perpendicular sides and all right angles.

Gray Squadron pilots can land on shapes with exactly 1 right angle.

Answer the questions.

Will the Green Squadron pilots land on any triangles? _____

Will the Yellow Squadron pilots land on any parallelograms? _____

Will the Red Squadron pilots land on any trapezoids? _____

Will the Gold Squadron pilots land on any squares? _____

Help guide the pilots by coloring the shapes
according to the squadron names.

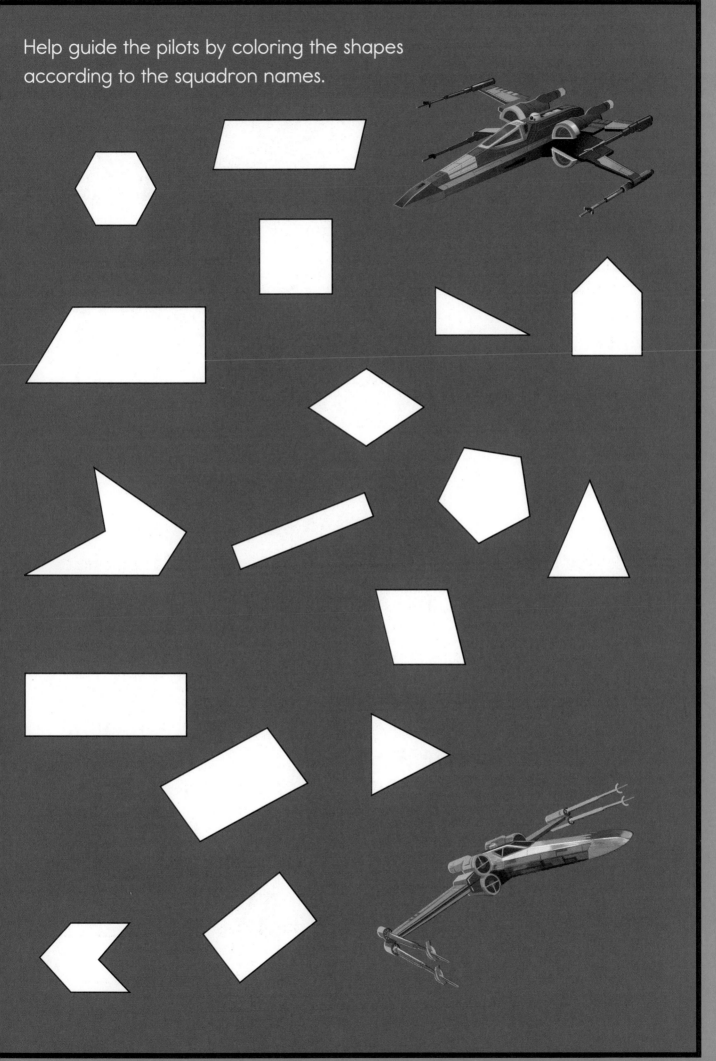

Symmetric Slices

A **line of symmetry** divides a shape into two parts that mirror each other exactly.

A shape can have zero, one, two, or more lines of symmetry.

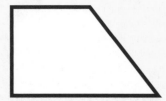

0 lines of symmetry

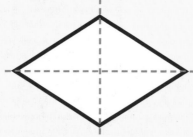

2 lines of symmetry

1 line of symmetry

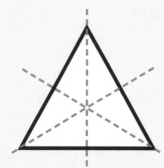

3 lines of symmetry

Was the shape sliced with a line of symmetry? Write **yes** or **no**. Next, draw all possible lines of symmetry in the blank for each shape. Then write the number of lines of symmetry.

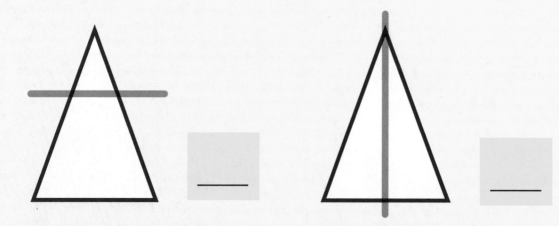

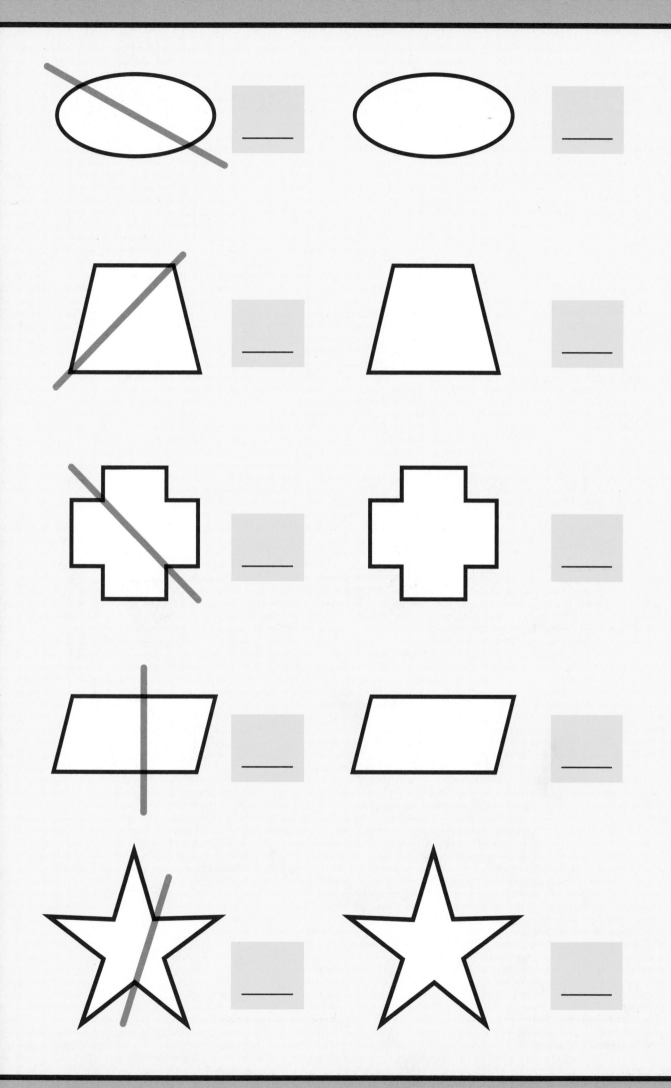

Colorful Commander

Add or **subtract**. Then use the key to color the spaces.

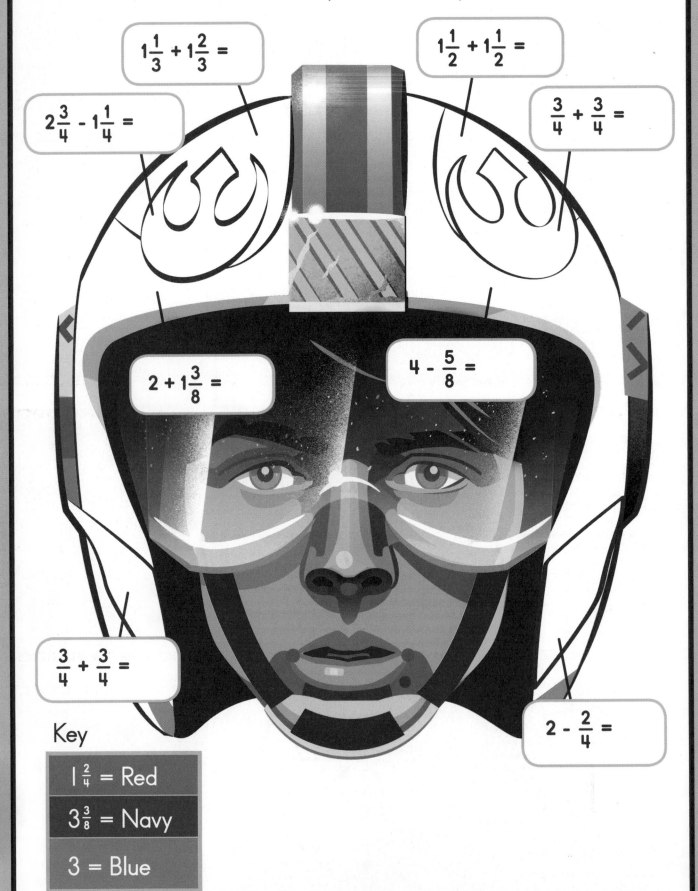

$1\frac{1}{3} + 1\frac{2}{3} =$

$1\frac{1}{2} + 1\frac{1}{2} =$

$2\frac{3}{4} - 1\frac{1}{4} =$

$\frac{3}{4} + \frac{3}{4} =$

$2 + 1\frac{3}{8} =$

$4 - \frac{5}{8} =$

$\frac{3}{4} + \frac{3}{4} =$

$2 - \frac{2}{4} =$

Key

$1\frac{2}{4}$ = Red

$3\frac{3}{8}$ = Navy

3 = Blue

Answers

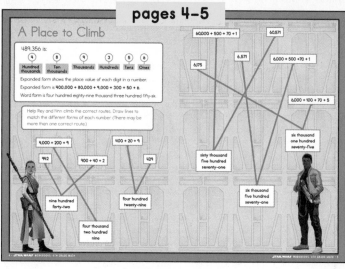

A Place to Climb

489,356 is:

4	8	9	3	5	6
Hundred thousands	Ten thousands	Thousands	Hundreds	Tens	Ones

Expanded form shows the place value of each digit in a number.
Expanded form is 400,000 + 80,000 + 9,000 + 300 + 50 + 6.
Word form is four hundred eighty-nine thousand three hundred fifty-six.

Help Rey and Finn climb the correct routes. Draw lines to match the different forms of each number. (There may be more than one correct route.)

60,000 + 500 + 70 + 1   60,571

6,571   6,000 + 500 + 70 + 1

6,175   6,000 + 100 + 70 + 5

4,000 + 200 + 9   400 + 20 + 9

942   900 + 40 + 2   429

six thousand one hundred seventy-five

sixty thousand five hundred seventy-one

six thousand five hundred seventy-one

nine hundred forty-two   four hundred twenty-nine

four thousand two hundred nine

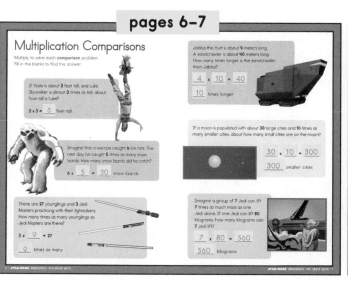

Multiplication Comparisons

Multiply to solve each comparison problem. Fill in the blanks to find the answer.

If Yoda is about 2 feet tall, and Luke Skywalker is almost 3 times as tall, about how tall is Luke?
2 x 3 = 6 feet tall

Imagine that a wampa caught 6 ice rats. The next day, he caught 5 times as many snow lizards. How many snow lizards did he catch?
6 x 5 = 30 snow lizards

There are 27 younglings and 3 Jedi Masters practicing with their lightsabers. How many times as many younglings as Jedi Masters are there?
3 x 9 = 27
9 times as many

Jabba the Hutt is about 4 meters long. A sandcrawler is about 40 meters long. How many times longer is the sandcrawler than Jabba?
4 x 10 = 40
10 times longer

If a moon is populated with about 30 large cities and 10 times as many smaller cities, about how many small cities are on the moon?
30 x 10 = 300
300 smaller cities

Imagine a group of 7 Jedi can lift 7 times as much mass as one Jedi alone. If one Jedi can lift 80 kilograms, how many kilograms can 7 Jedi lift?
7 x 80 = 560
560 kilograms

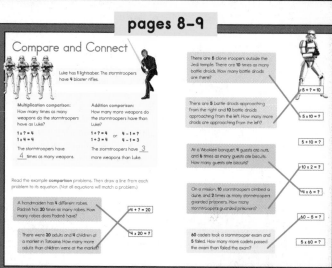

Compare and Connect

Luke has 1 lightsaber. The stormtroopers have 4 blaster rifles.

Multiplication comparison:
How many times as many weapons do the stormtroopers have as Luke?
1 x ? = 4
1 x 4 = 4
The stormtroopers have 4 times as many weapons.

Addition comparison:
How many more weapons do the stormtroopers have than Luke?
1 + ? = 4   or   4 – 1 = ?
1 + 3 = 4   4 – 1 = 3
The stormtroopers have 3 more weapons than Luke.

Read the example comparison problems. Then draw a line from each problem to its equation. (Not all equations will match a problem.)

A handmaiden has 4 different robes. Padmé has 20 times as many robes. How many robes does Padmé have?

There were 20 adults and 4 children at a market in Tatooine. How many more adults than children were at the market?

4 + ? = 20
4 x 20 = ?

There are 5 clone troopers outside the Jedi temple. There are 10 times as many battle droids. How many battle droids are there?

There are 5 battle droids approaching from the right and 10 battle droids approaching from the left. How many more droids are approaching from the left?

At a Wookiee banquet, 4 guests ate nuts, and 6 times as many guests ate biscuits. How many guests ate biscuits?

On a mission, 10 stormtroopers climbed a dune, and 2 times as many stormtroopers guarded prisoners. How many stormtroopers guarded prisoners?

60 cadets took a stormtrooper exam and 5 failed. How many more cadets passed the exam than failed the exam?

5 + ? = 10
5 x 10 = ?
5 + 10 = ?
10 x 2 = ?
4 x 6 = ?
60 – 5 = ?
5 x 60 = ?

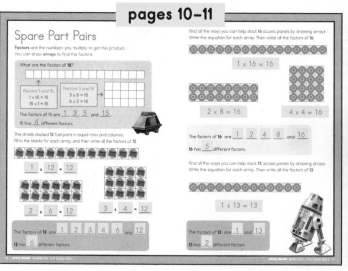

Spare Part Pairs

Factors are the numbers you multiply to get the product. You can draw arrays to find the factors.

What are the factors of 15?

Factors 1 and 15:
1 x 15 = 15
15 x 1 = 15

Factors 3 and 5:
3 x 5 = 15
5 x 3 = 15

The factors of 15 are 1, 3, 5, and 15.
15 has 4 different factors.

The droids stacked 12 fuel ports in equal rows and columns. Fill in the blanks for each array, and then write all the factors of 12.

1 x 12 = 12
2 x 6 = 12
3 x 4 = 12

The factors of 12 are 1, 2, 3, 4, 6, and 12.
12 has 6 different factors.

Find all the ways you can help stack 16 access panels by drawing arrays. Write the equation for each array. Then write all the factors of 16.

1 x 16 = 16
2 x 8 = 16
4 x 4 = 16

The factors of 16 are 1, 2, 4, 8, and 16.
16 has 5 different factors.

Find all the ways you can help stack 13 access panels by drawing arrays. Write the equation for each array. Then write all the factors of 13.

1 x 13 = 13

The factors of 13 are 1 and 13.
13 has 2 different factors.

Prime Territory

A prime number has only two factors. The number 5 is a prime number. Its factors are 1 and 5. A composite number has three or more factors. The number 51 is a composite number. Its factors are 1, 3, 17, and 51.

Imagine that you have discovered a new planet. Creatures roam over the land and water. The harmless creatures are marked with prime numbers. The dangerous creatures are marked with composite numbers. Circle the harmless creatures. Cross out the dangerous creatures.

42, 6, 2, 63, 17, 71, 19, 12, 25, 3, 20, 23

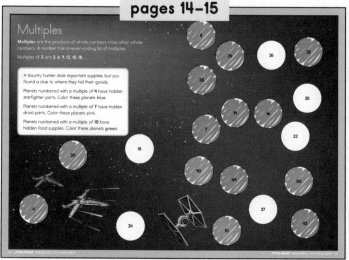

Multiples

Multiples are the products of whole numbers times other whole numbers. A number has a never-ending list of multiples.
Multiples of 3 are 3, 6, 9, 12, 15, 18, ...

A bounty hunter stole important supplies, but you found a clue to where they hid their goods.

Planets numbered with a multiple of 4 have hidden starfighter parts. Color these planets blue.

Planets numbered with a multiple of 7 have hidden droid parts. Color these planets pink.

Planets numbered with a multiple of 10 have hidden food supplies. Color these planets green.

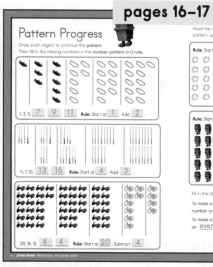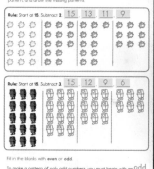

Pattern Progress

Draw each object to continue the pattern. Then fill in the missing numbers in the number pattern and rule.

1, 3, 5, 7, 9, 11   Rule: Start at 1. Add 2.

4, 7, 10, 13, 16   Rule: Start at 4. Add 3.

20, 16, 12, 8, 4   Rule: Start at 20. Subtract 4.

Read the rule below. Then fill in the missing numbers in the number pattern, and draw the missing patterns.

Rule: Start at 15. Subtract 2.   15, 13, 11, 9

Rule: Start at 15. Subtract 3.   15, 12, 9, 6

Fill in the blanks with even or odd.

To make a pattern of only odd numbers, you must begin with an odd number and odd or subtract an even number.

To make a pattern that shows only even numbers, you must begin with an even number, and add or subtract an even number.

Answers

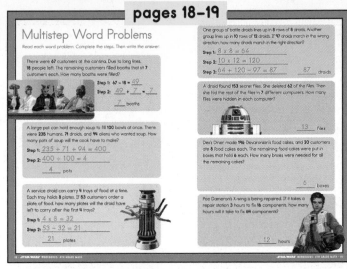

pages 18–19

Multistep Word Problems

Read each word problem. Complete the steps. Then write the answer.

There were 67 customers at the cantina. Due to long lines, 18 people left. The remaining customers filled booths that sit 7 customers each. How many booths were filled?

Step 1: 67 – 18 = __49__
Step 2: 49 ÷ 7 = __7__

__7__ booths

A large pot can hold enough soup to fill 100 bowls at once. There were 235 humans, 71 droids, and 94 aliens who wanted soup. How many pots of soup will the cook have to make?

Step 1: __235 + 71 + 94 = 400__
Step 2: __400 ÷ 100 = 4__

__4__ pots

A service droid can carry 4 trays of food at a time. Each tray holds 8 plates. If 53 customers order a plate of food, how many plates will the droid have left to carry after the first 4 trays?

Step 1: __4 x 8 = 32__
Step 2: __53 – 32 = 21__

__21__ plates

One group of battle droids lines up in 8 rows of 8 droids. Another group lines up in 10 rows of 12 droids. If 97 droids march in the wrong direction, how many droids march in the right direction?

Step 1: $8 \times 8 = 64$
Step 2: $10 \times 12 = 120$
Step 3: $64 + 120 - 97 = 87$

__87__ droids

A droid found 153 secret files. She deleted 62 of the files. Then she hid the rest of the files in 7 different computers. How many files were hidden in each computer?

__13__ files

Dex's Diner made 196 Devaronian's food cakes, and 20 customers ate 8 food cakes each. The remaining food cakes were put in boxes that hold 6 each. How many boxes were needed for all the remaining cakes?

__6__ boxes

Poe Dameron's X-wing is being repaired. If it takes a repair station 3 hours to fix 16 components, how many hours will it take to fix 64 components?

__12__ hours

pages 20–21

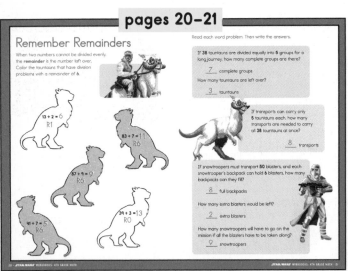

Remember Remainders

When two numbers cannot be divided evenly, the **remainder** is the number left over. Color the tauntauns that have division problems with a remainder of 6.

13 ÷ 2 = 6
R1

83 ÷ 7 = 11
R6

87 ÷ 9 = 9
R6

41 ÷ 7 = 5
R6

39 ÷ 3 = 13
R0

Read each word problem. Then write the answers.

If 38 tauntauns are divided equally into 5 groups for a long journey, how many complete groups are there?

__7__ complete groups

How many tauntauns are left over?

__3__ tauntauns

If transports can carry only 5 tauntauns each, how many transports are needed to carry all 38 tauntauns at once?

__8__ transports

If snowtroopers must transport 50 blasters, and each snowtrooper's backpack can hold 6 blasters, how many backpacks can they fill?

__8__ full backpacks

How many extra blasters would be left?

__2__ extra blasters

How many snowtroopers will have to go on the mission if all the blasters have to be taken along?

__9__ snowtroopers

pages 22–23

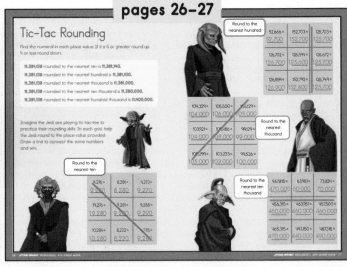

Millions of Stars

The **place value** of a digit in a number is determined by where it appears in the number. Each place value is 10 times the value of the place to its right, and 100 times the value of the place two places to its right, and so on.

The meaning of 7,777,777 is:

7 x 1,000,000	7 x 100,000	7 x 10,000	7 x 1,000	7 x 100	7 x 10	7
Millions	Hundred thousands	Ten thousands	Thousands	Hundreds	Tens	Ones

Use hyperdrive to jump forward and back along the place value chart to fill in the blanks.

7 x 100 = __700__
7,000 x 10 = __70,000__
7,000 x 100 = __700,000__
7 x 1,000 = __7,000__
77 x 10 = __770__
700 ÷ 100 = __7__
70,000 ÷ 1,000 = __70__
7,000 ÷ 100 = __70__
770 ÷ 10 = __77__

Multiply or divide on each star.

300 x 10 =
__3,000__

62 x 10 =
__620__

300 ÷ 10 =
__30__

417 x 100 =
__41,700__

417,000 ÷ 10 =
__41,700__

62 x 100 =
__6,200__

123,400 ÷ 100 =
__1,234__

1,234 x 10 =
__12,340__

pages 24–25

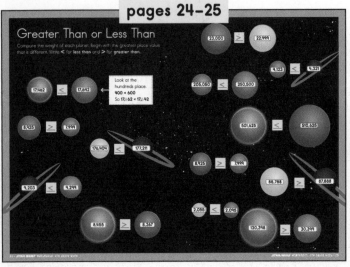

Greater Than or Less Than

Compare the weight of each planet. Begin with the greatest place value that is different. Write **<** for **less than** and **>** for **greater than**.

23,000 > 22,999

4,123 < 4,321

17,462 < 17,642

Look at the hundreds place.
400 < 600
So 17,462 < 17,642

205,050 < 250,500

501,625 < 510,625

8,325 > 7,499

176,404 < 177,211

8,325 > 7,499

86,788 > 87,888

9,203 < 9,299

2,055 < 2,045

8,455 > 8,267

130,348 > 303,799

pages 26–27

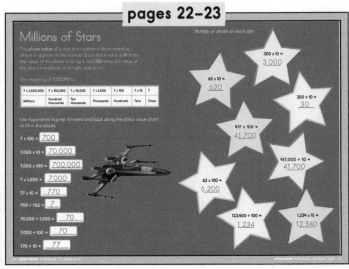

Tic-Tac Rounding

Find the numeral in each place value. If it is 5 or greater round up. 4 or less round down.

11,381,138 rounded to the nearest ten is 11,381,140.
11,381,138 rounded to the nearest hundred is 11,381,100.
11,381,138 rounded to the nearest thousand is 11,381,000.
11,381,138 rounded to the nearest ten thousand is 11,380,000.
11,381,138 rounded to the nearest hundred thousand is 11,400,000.

Imagine the Jedi are playing tic-tac-toe to practice their rounding skills. In each grid, help the Jedi round to the place value provided. Draw a line to connect the same numbers and win.

Round to the nearest hundred

52,666 = 52,700	152,703 = 152,700	125,703 = 125,700
126,702 = 126,700	126,594 = 125,600	126,672 = 125,700
126,894 = 126,900	152,792 = 152,800	125,749 = 125,700

Round to the nearest thousand

104,324 = 104,000	105,500 = 105,000	105,029 = 105,000
103,921 = 104,000	100,486 = 105,000	99,123 = 99,000
105,099 = 105,000	103,233 = 103,000	99,536 = 100,000

Round to the nearest ten

9,276 = 9,280	8,281 = 8,280	9,272 = 9,270
19,276 = 19,280	9,281 = 9,280	9,288 = 9,290
10,284 = 10,280	8,222 = 8,220	9,275 = 9,280

Round to the nearest ten thousand

467,815 = 470,000	63,951 = 60,000	73,824 = 70,000
456,315 = 460,000	463,951 = 460,000	457,500 = 460,000
466,315 = 470,000	443,150 = 440,000	487,318 = 490,000

pages 28–29

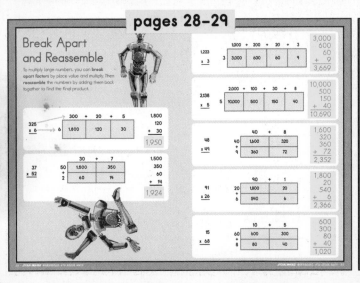

Break Apart and Reassemble

To multiply large numbers, you can **break apart factors** by place value and multiply. Then **reassemble** the numbers by adding them back together to find the final product.

325
x 6

| | 300 | + | 20 | + | 5 |
| 6 | 1,800 | | 120 | | 30 |

1,800
120
+ 30
1,950

37
x 52

	30	+	7
50	1,500		350
2	60		14

1,500
350
60
+ 14
1,924

1,223
x 3

| | 1,000 | + | 200 | + | 20 | + | 3 |
| 3 | 3,000 | | 600 | | 60 | | 9 |

3,000
600
60
+ 9
3,669

2,138
x 5

| | 2,000 | + | 100 | + | 30 | + | 8 |
| 5 | 10,000 | | 500 | | 150 | | 40 |

10,000
500
150
+ 40
10,690

48
x 49

	40	+	8
40	1,600		320
9	360		72

1,600
320
360
+ 72
2,352

91
x 26

	90	+	1
20	1,800		20
6	540		6

1,800
20
540
+ 6
2,366

15
x 68

	10	+	5
60	600		300
8	80		40

600
300
80
+ 40
1,020

pages 30–31

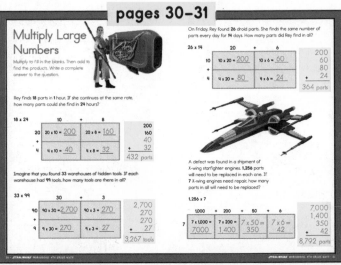

Multiply Large Numbers

Multiply to fill in the blanks. Then add to find the products. Write a complete answer to the question.

Rey finds 18 parts in 1 hour. If she continues at the same rate, how many parts could she find in 24 hours?

18 x 24

	20	+	4
20	20 x 10 = 200		20 x 8 = 160
4	4 x 10 = 40		4 x 8 = 32

200
160
40
+ 32
432 parts

Imagine that you found 33 warehouses of hidden tools. If each warehouse had 99 tools, how many tools are there in all?

33 x 99

	30	+	3
90	90 x 30 = 2,700		90 x 3 = 270
9	9 x 30 = 270		9 x 3 = 27

2,700
270
270
+ 27
3,267 tools

On Friday, Rey found 26 droid parts. She finds the same number of parts every day for 14 days. How many parts did Rey find in all?

26 x 14

	20	+	6
10	10 x 20 = 200		10 x 6 = 60
4	4 x 20 = 80		4 x 6 = 24

200
60
80
+ 24
364 parts

A defect was found in a shipment of X-wing starfighter engines. 1,256 parts will need to be replaced in each one. If 7 x-wing engines need repair, how many parts in all will need to be replaced?

1,256 x 7

| | 1,000 | + | 200 | + | 50 | + | 6 |
| 7 | 7 x 1,000 = 7,000 | | 7 x 200 = 1,400 | | 7 x 50 = 350 | | 7 x 6 = 42 |

7,000
1,400
350
+ 42
8,792 parts

pages 32-33

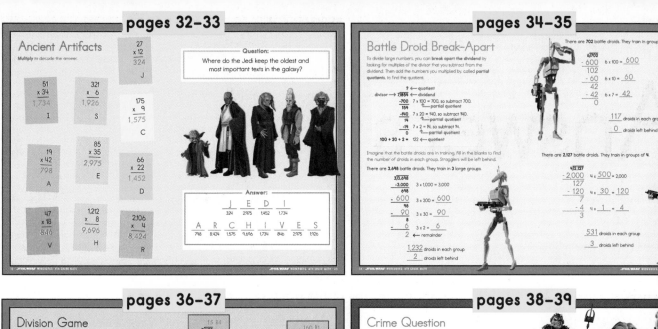

Ancient Artifacts

Multiply to decode the answer.

$$27 \times 12 = 324 \quad \text{J}$$

$51 \times 34 = 1,734$ — I	$321 \times 6 = 1,926$ — S

$$175 \times 9 = 1,575 \quad \text{C}$$

$19 \times 42 = 798$ — A	$85 \times 35 = 2,975$ — E

$$66 \times 22 = 1,452 \quad \text{D}$$

$47 \times 18 = 846$ — V	$1,212 \times 8 = 9,696$ — H

$$2,106 \times 4 = 8,424 \quad \text{R}$$

Question:
Where do the Jedi keep the oldest and most important texts in the galaxy?

Answer:
J E D I
A R C H I V E S
798 8,424 1,575 9,696 1,734 846 2,975 1,926

pages 34-35

Battle Droid Break-Apart

To divide large numbers, you can **break apart the dividend** by looking for multiples of the divisor that you subtract from the dividend. Then add the numbers you multiplied by, called **partial quotients**, to find the quotient.

There are 702 battle droids. They train in groups of 6.

$$6\overline{)702}$$
$$-600 \quad 6 \times 100 = 600$$
$$102$$
$$-60 \quad 6 \times 10 = 60$$
$$42$$
$$-42 \quad 6 \times 7 = 42$$
$$0$$

117 droids in each group
0 droids left behind

Imagine that the battle droids are in training. Fill in the blanks to find the number of droids in each group. Stragglers will be left behind.

There are 3,698 battle droids. They train in 3 large groups.

$$3\overline{)3,698}$$
$$-3,000 \quad 3 \times 1,000 = 3,000$$
$$698$$
$$-600 \quad 3 \times 200 = 600$$
$$98$$
$$-90 \quad 3 \times 30 = 90$$
$$8$$
$$-6 \quad 3 \times 2 = 6$$
$$2 \quad \leftarrow \text{remainder}$$

1,232 droids in each group
2 droids left behind

There are 2,127 battle droids. They train in groups of 4.

$$4\overline{)2,127}$$
$$-2,000 \quad 4 \times 500 = 2,000$$
$$127$$
$$-120 \quad 4 \times 30 = 120$$
$$7$$
$$-4 \quad 4 \times 1 = 4$$
$$3$$

531 droids in each group
3 droids left behind

pages 36-37

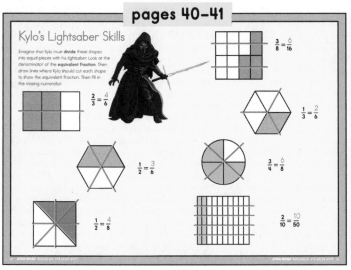

Division Game

Divide each problem. Then color the boxes that have the same remainder with a matching color. To win the game, circle the box without a match.

pages 38-39

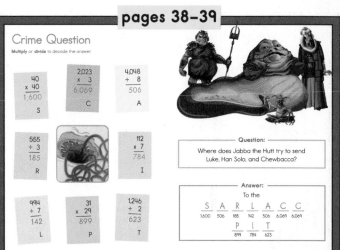

Crime Question

Multiply or divide to decode the answer.

$40 \times 40 = 1,600$ — S	$2,023 \times 3 = 6,069$ — C	$4,048 \div 8 = 506$ — A
$555 \div 3 = 185$ — R		$112 \times 7 = 784$ — I
$994 \div 7 = 142$ — L	$31 \times 29 = 899$ — P	$1,246 \div 2 = 623$ — T

Question:
Where does Jabba the Hutt try to send Luke, Han Solo, and Chewbacca?

Answer:
To the
S A R L A C C
1,600 506 185 142 506 6,069 6,069
P I T
899 784 623

pages 40-41

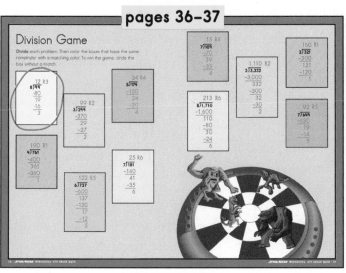

Kylo's Lightsaber Skills

Imagine that Kylo must **divide** these shapes into equal pieces with his lightsaber. Look at the denominator of the **equivalent fraction**. Then draw lines where Kylo should cut each shape to show the equivalent fraction. Then fill in the missing numerator.

$$\frac{2}{3} = \frac{4}{6} \qquad \frac{3}{8} = \frac{6}{16} \qquad \frac{1}{3} = \frac{2}{6}$$

$$\frac{1}{2} = \frac{3}{6} \qquad \frac{3}{4} = \frac{6}{8}$$

$$\frac{1}{2} = \frac{4}{8} \qquad \frac{2}{10} = \frac{10}{50}$$

pages 42-43

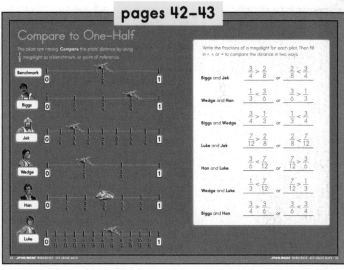

Compare to One-Half

The pilots are racing. **Compare** the pilots' distance by using $\frac{1}{2}$ megalight as a benchmark, or point of reference.

Write the fractions of a megalight for each pilot. Then fill in <, >, or = to compare the distance in two ways.

Biggs and Jek	$\frac{3}{4} > \frac{2}{8}$	or	$\frac{2}{8} < \frac{3}{4}$
Wedge and Han	$\frac{1}{3} < \frac{3}{6}$	or	$\frac{3}{6} > \frac{1}{3}$
Biggs and Wedge	$\frac{3}{4} > \frac{1}{3}$	or	$\frac{1}{3} < \frac{3}{4}$
Luke and Jek	$\frac{7}{12} > \frac{2}{8}$	or	$\frac{2}{8} < \frac{7}{12}$
Han and Luke	$\frac{3}{6} < \frac{7}{12}$	or	$\frac{7}{12} > \frac{3}{6}$
Wedge and Luke	$\frac{1}{3} < \frac{7}{12}$	or	$\frac{7}{12} > \frac{1}{3}$
Biggs and Han	$\frac{3}{4} > \frac{3}{6}$	or	$\frac{3}{6} < \frac{3}{4}$

pages 44-45

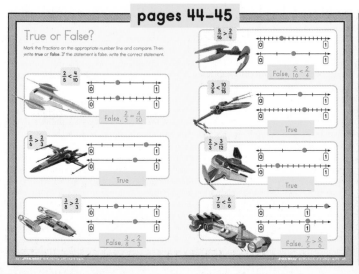

True or False?

Mark the fractions on the appropriate number line and compare. Then write **true** or **false**. If the statement is false, write the correct statement.

$$\frac{2}{5} < \frac{4}{10} \qquad \text{False, } \frac{2}{5} = \frac{4}{10}$$

$$\frac{5}{6} > \frac{2}{3} \qquad \text{True}$$

$$\frac{3}{8} > \frac{2}{3} \qquad \text{False, } \frac{3}{8} < \frac{2}{3}$$

$$\frac{5}{16} < \frac{2}{4} \qquad \text{False, } \frac{5}{16} < \frac{2}{4}$$

$$\frac{3}{5} < \frac{10}{15} \qquad \text{True}$$

$$\frac{2}{3} > \frac{3}{12} \qquad \text{True}$$

$$\frac{7}{5} < \frac{6}{5} \qquad \text{False, } \frac{7}{5} > \frac{6}{5}$$

pages 46-47

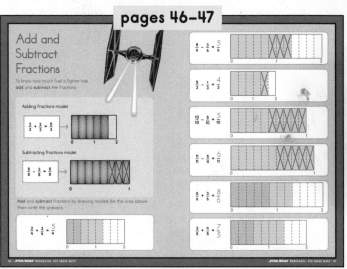

Add and Subtract Fractions

To know how much fuel a fighter has, **add** and **subtract** the fractions.

Adding fractions model

$$\frac{3}{3} + \frac{2}{3} = \frac{5}{3}$$

Subtracting fractions model

$$\frac{8}{5} - \frac{3}{5} = \frac{5}{5}$$

Add and subtract fractions by drawing models like the ones above. Then write the answers.

$$\frac{2}{4} + \frac{3}{4} = \frac{5}{4}$$

$$\frac{8}{6} - \frac{3}{6} = \frac{5}{6}$$

$$\frac{5}{3} - \frac{1}{3} = \frac{4}{3}$$

$$\frac{10}{10} - \frac{5}{10} = \frac{5}{10}$$

$$\frac{11}{11} - \frac{5}{11} = \frac{6}{11}$$

$$\frac{5}{8} + \frac{3}{8} = \frac{8}{8}$$

$$\frac{3}{5} + \frac{4}{5} = \frac{7}{5}$$

Answers

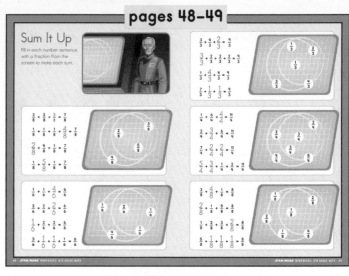

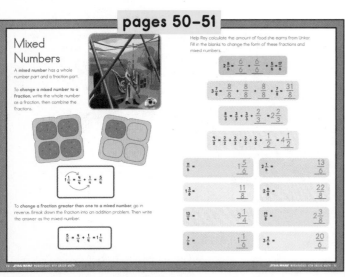

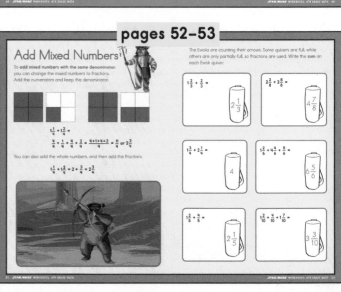

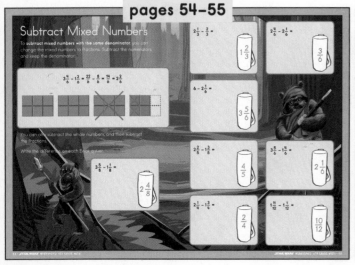

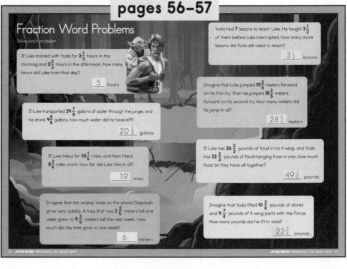

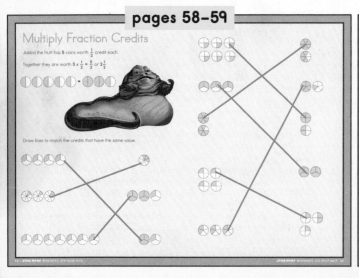

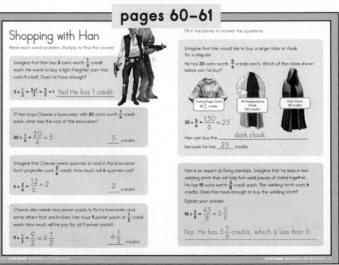

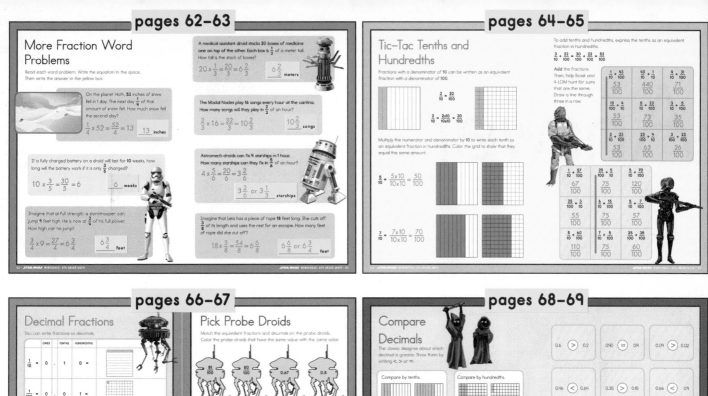

pages 62-63

More Fraction Word Problems

Read each word problem. Write the equation in the space. Then write the answer in the yellow box.

On the planet Hoth, 52 inches of snow fell in 1 day. The next day $\frac{1}{4}$ of that amount of snow fell. How much snow fell the second day?

$\frac{1}{4} \times 52 = \frac{52}{4} = 13$ **13 inches**

If a fully charged battery on a droid will last for 10 weeks, how long will the battery work if it is only $\frac{3}{5}$ charged?

$10 \times \frac{3}{5} = \frac{30}{5} = 6$ **6 weeks**

Imagine that at full strength, a stormtrooper can jump 9 feet high. He is now at $\frac{3}{4}$ of his full power. How high can he jump?

$\frac{3}{4} \times 9 = \frac{27}{4} = 6\frac{3}{4}$ **6$\frac{3}{4}$ feet**

A medical assistant droid stacks 20 boxes of medicine one on top of the other. Each box is $\frac{1}{3}$ of a meter tall. How tall is the stack of boxes?

$20 \times \frac{1}{3} = \frac{20}{3} = 6\frac{2}{3}$ **6$\frac{2}{3}$ meters**

The Modal Nodes play 16 songs every hour at the cantina. How many songs will they play in $\frac{2}{3}$ of an hour?

$\frac{2}{3} \times 16 = \frac{32}{3} = 10\frac{2}{3}$ **10$\frac{2}{3}$ songs**

Astromech droids can fix 4 starships in 1 hour. How many starships can they fix in $\frac{5}{6}$ of an hour?

$4 \times \frac{5}{6} = \frac{20}{6} = 3\frac{2}{6}$ **3$\frac{2}{6}$ or 3$\frac{1}{3}$ starships**

Imagine that Leia has a piece of rope 18 feet long. She cuts off $\frac{3}{8}$ of its length and uses the rest for an escape. How many feet of rope did she cut off?

$18 \times \frac{3}{8} = \frac{54}{8} = 6\frac{6}{8}$ **6$\frac{6}{8}$ or 6$\frac{3}{4}$ feet**

pages 64-65

Tic-Tac Tenths and Hundredths

Fractions with a denominator of 10 can be written as an equivalent fraction with a denominator of 100.

$\frac{2}{10} = \frac{20}{100}$

$\frac{2}{10} = \frac{2 \times 10}{10 \times 10} = \frac{20}{100}$

Multiply the numerator and denominator by 10 to write each tenth as an equivalent fraction in hundredths. Color the grid to show that they equal the same amount.

$\frac{5}{10} = \frac{5 \times 10}{10 \times 10} = \frac{50}{100}$

$\frac{7}{10} = \frac{7 \times 10}{10 \times 10} = \frac{70}{100}$

To add tenths and hundredths, express the tenths as an equivalent fraction in hundredths.

$\frac{3}{10} + \frac{22}{100} = \frac{30}{100} + \frac{22}{100} = \frac{52}{100}$

Add the fractions. Then, help Bossk and 4-LOM hunt for sums that are the same. Draw a line through three in a row.

$\frac{1}{10} + \frac{43}{100} = \frac{53}{100}$	$\frac{43}{100} + \frac{1}{10} = \frac{440}{100}$	$\frac{4}{10} + \frac{31}{100} = \frac{71}{100}$
$\frac{1}{10} + \frac{4}{100} = \frac{53}{100}$	$\frac{5}{100} + \frac{1}{100} = \frac{73}{100}$	$\frac{3}{10} + \frac{5}{100} = \frac{35}{100}$
$\frac{3}{10} + \frac{23}{100} = \frac{53}{100}$	$\frac{23}{10} + \frac{4}{100} = \frac{63}{100}$	$\frac{3}{10} + \frac{2}{100} = \frac{26}{100}$

$\frac{1}{10} + \frac{57}{100} = \frac{67}{100}$	$\frac{25}{100} + \frac{5}{10} = \frac{75}{100}$	$\frac{5}{10} + \frac{70}{100} = \frac{120}{100}$
$\frac{25}{100} + \frac{3}{10} = \frac{55}{100}$	$\frac{6}{10} + \frac{15}{100} = \frac{75}{100}$	$\frac{5}{10} + \frac{7}{100} = \frac{57}{100}$
$\frac{5}{10} + \frac{60}{100} = \frac{110}{100}$	$\frac{7}{10} + \frac{5}{100} = \frac{75}{100}$	$\frac{25}{100} + \frac{35}{100} = \frac{60}{100}$

pages 66-67

Decimal Fractions

You can write fractions as decimals.

	ONES	TENTHS	HUNDREDTHS
$\frac{1}{10} =$	0	1	0
$\frac{1}{100} =$	0	0	1
$\frac{101}{100} =$	1	0	1

Color the grid to show 0.62.

$0.62 = \frac{62}{100}$

Color the grids to show 1.25.

$1.25 = \frac{125}{100}$

Pick Probe Droids

Match the equivalent fractions and decimals on the probe droids. Color the probe droids that have the same value with the same color.

$\frac{81}{100}$ $\frac{50}{100}$ 0.67 0.5

$\frac{67}{100}$ $\frac{16}{100}$ 1.06 0.81

$\frac{106}{100}$ $\frac{5}{10}$ 1.16 0.50

pages 68-69

Compare Decimals

The Jawas disagree about which decimal is greater. Show them by writing <, > or =.

Compare by tenths.

$0.3 < 0.7$

Compare by hundredths.

$0.27 > 0.03$

Compare tenths and hundredths by making tenths into hundredths.

$0.3 > 0.22$ $0.30 > 0.22$

$0.6 > 0.2$ $0.90 = 0.9$ $0.09 > 0.02$

$0.46 < 0.64$ $0.35 > 0.15$ $0.66 < 0.9$

$0.7 < 0.77$ $0.1 < 0.11$ $0.47 < 0.7$

$0.4 < 0.9$ $0.9 > 0.89$ $0.8 = 0.80$

$0.3 < 0.53$ $0.1 > 0.01$

pages 70-71

Colorful Decimal Fractions

Imagine that C-3PO is working on a new circuit board. Use the **four** different colors to color the **hundredths** circuit board any way you wish.

SAMPLE ANSWER

Use **five** different colors to color another hundredths circuit board any way you wish.

SAMPLE ANSWER

Each color represents a different hundredths decimal. Fill in the key to show what decimal each color represents.

Color 1:	yellow	= Decimal 0.32
Color 2:	green	= Decimal 0.36
Color 3:	blue	= Decimal 0.12
Color 4:	red	= Decimal 0.20

SAMPLE ANSWERS

Write the decimals in order from least to greatest.

0.12, 0.20, 0.32, 0.36

Each color represents a different hundredths decimal. Fill in the key to show what decimal each color represents.

Color 1:	blue	= Decimal 0.13
Color 2:	yellow	= Decimal 0.17
Color 3:	pink	= Decimal 0.29
Color 4:	green	= Decimal 0.15
Color 5:	purple	= Decimal 0.26

SAMPLE ANSWERS

Write the decimals in order from greatest to least.

0.29, 0.26, 0.17, 0.15, 0.13

pages 72-73

Area and Perimeter Formulas

The **area** of a rectangle is the number of square units that cover a region. Area is measured in square units.

Area = Length x Width
$A = L \times W$

The **perimeter** of a rectangle is the total length of its sides.

Perimeter = Length + Width + Length + Width
$P = L + W + L + W$
$P = (2 \times L) + (2 \times W)$
$P = 2 \times (L + W)$

Fill in the blanks in the formulas to find each answer.

Imagine that the clone troopers have stormed aboard a captured ship. What is the **area** of the cargo hold that they must search?

$A = 31 \times 25 = 775$ square feet

Imagine that the **area** of the clone troopers' weapon room is 162 square meters. What is the **length** of the missing side of the room?

$A = L \times 9 = 162$
$A = 18 \times 9 = 162$
$L = 18$ meters

Imagine that Jango is watching a clone cadet squad during training. What is the **perimeter** of the square bay they are gathered in?

$P = 30 + 30 + 30 + 30$
$P = 120$ meters

Imagine that the clone troopers are in a training formation, and the **area** of their formation is 36 meters. What is the **length** of their formation?

$A = L \times 4 = 36$
$A = 9 \times 4 = 36$
$L = 9$ meters

pages 74-75

Rebel Surprises

Use **area** and **perimeter** formulas with length (l) and width (w) to find the missing dimension. Then use the key to color the rebel targets.

Key:
5 =
9 =
30 =
10 =

$l = 10$, $w = 5$ → $P = 30$

$l = 3$, $w = 2$ → $P = 10$

$l = 15$, $w = 2$ → $A = 30$

$l = 6\frac{1}{2}$, $w = 2$ → $A = 13$

$l = 20$, $w = \frac{1}{2}$ → $A = 10$

$l = 7$, $w = 6$ → $A = 42$

$l = 21$, $w = 8\frac{1}{2}$ → $P = 59$

$l = 12$, $w = 9$ → $P = 42$

$l = 6$, $w = 5\frac{5}{8}$

$l = 15$, $w = 1\frac{1}{2}$

$l = 4$

$P = 14$, $w = 3$

$P = 24$, $w = 3$

$l = 9$

pages 76-77

Meteorites on Endor

Imagine that the Ewoks have just found the remains of a meteor shower on Endor. They have picked up the following meteorites.

A meteorite $4\frac{1}{4}$ cm long.
A meteorite $5\frac{1}{4}$ cm long.
A meteorite 5 cm long.
A meteorite $5\frac{1}{4}$ cm long.
A meteorite $4\frac{1}{4}$ cm long.
A meteorite $4\frac{3}{4}$ cm long.

The line plot below shows the data from a meteor shower the year before. Draw Xs to include this year's data on the line plot.

Length of Meteorites Found

Fill in the blanks using data from the line plot.

How many meteorites were found in all? 11

The longest meteorite found was $5\frac{1}{4}$ centimeters.

The shortest meteorite was $1\frac{1}{4}$ centimeters shorter than the longest meteorite.

An Ewok finds a new meteorite $6\frac{3}{4}$ centimeters long. How much longer is that than the longest meteorite found so far?

$1\frac{1}{4}$ or $1\frac{1}{2}$ centimeters

Another Ewok finds a new meteorite $1\frac{3}{4}$ centimeters longer than the shortest meteorite length on the line plot. How long is it?

$5\frac{3}{4}$ centimeters

The new meteorites will change the line plot. What numbers do you have to add to the scale at the bottom of the line plot?

$5\frac{1}{2}$, $5\frac{3}{4}$, 6, $6\frac{1}{4}$, $6\frac{1}{2}$, $6\frac{3}{4}$

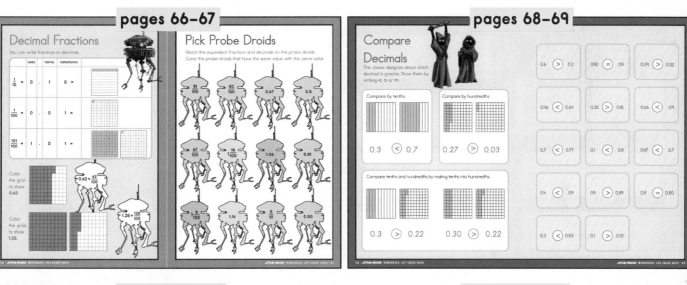
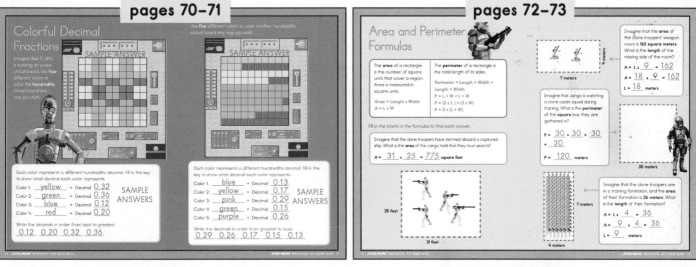
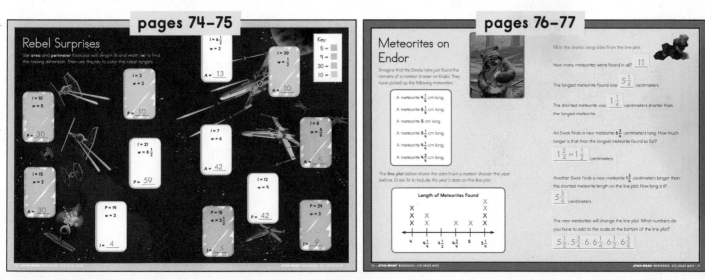

Answers

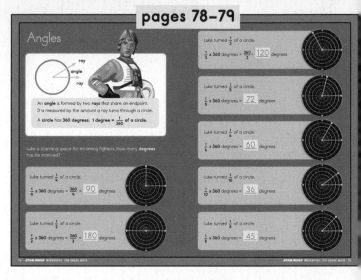

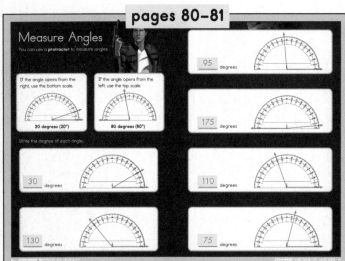

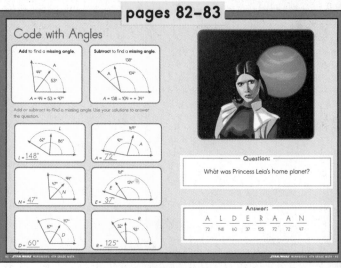

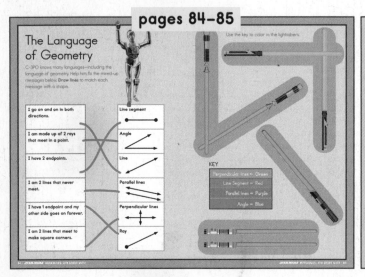

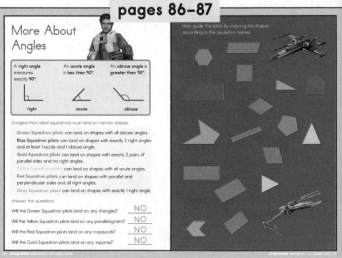

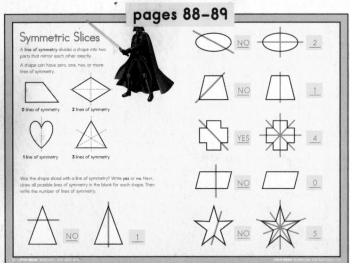